P[illegible] of a Lifetime

An Autobiography

A Collection of
Poems and Quotations

written by
Emil S. Saint Pellicer
qui est aussi
Marcel Toussaint

with narration by
Linda Dahlheimer

Published by NACG Press, a division of North American Consulting Group, Inc.

Printed in the United States of America

ISBN: 978-0-9623018-6-5

Library of Congress Control Number: 2009927988

To contact the author:
e-mail: marcel.toussaint@yahoo.com
website: www.marceltoussaint.com

To contact the publisher:
e-mail: charlesd@nacgonline.com
website: www.nacgpress.com

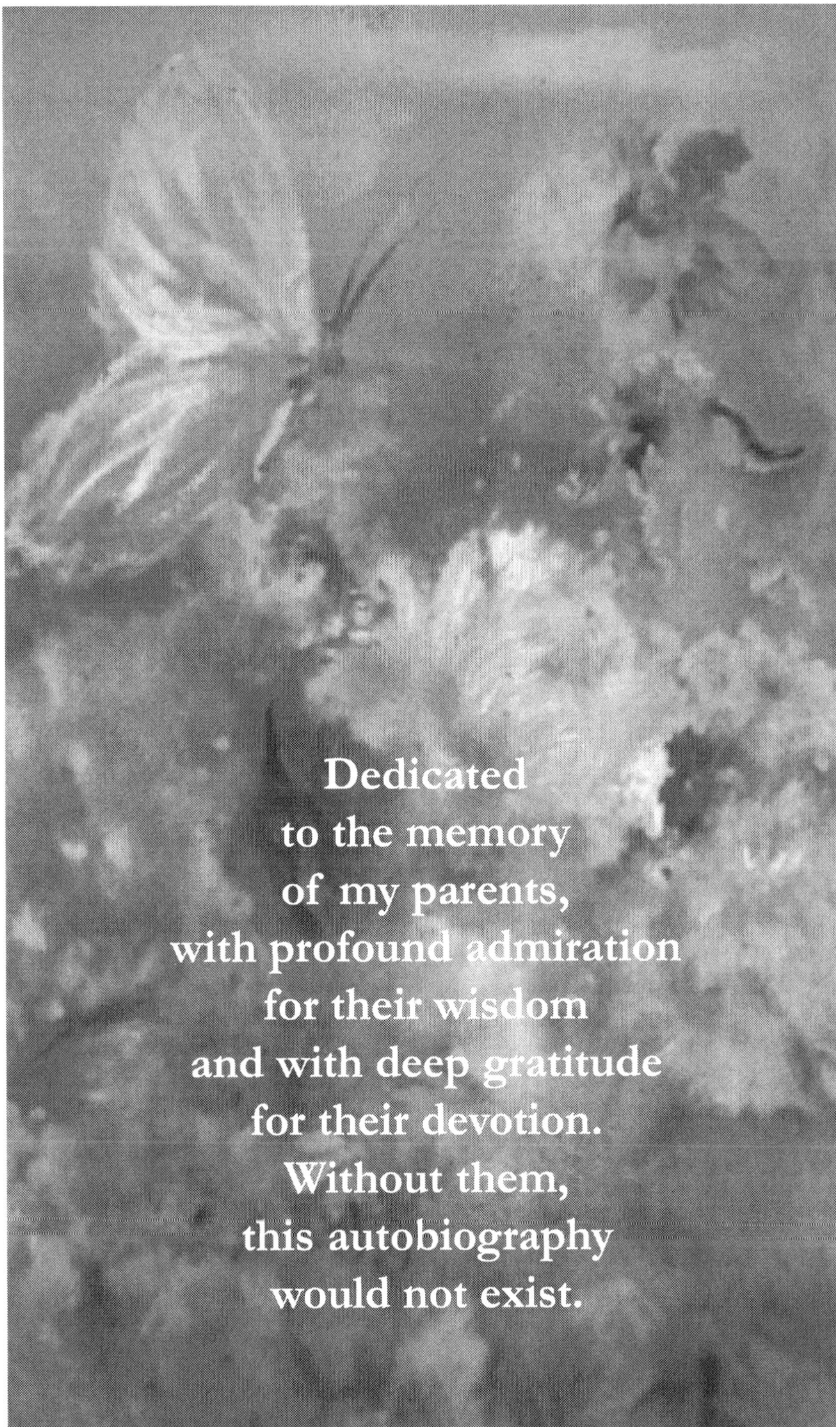

Dedicated
to the memory
of my parents,
with profound admiration
for their wisdom
and with deep gratitude
for their devotion.
Without them,
this autobiography
would not exist.

Acknowledgments

Charles Dahlheimer, noted author and lecturer, who was instrumental in layout, and publishing, and who assisted in editing.

Josephine Carter, the author's sister, with whom he collaborated on childhood recollections.

Seema Mukhi Dahlheimer, who was a consultant in the planning of this project. She holds an M.F.A. in Creative Writing.

Jeanne Wolff, whose sketches are found throughout the book. They are part of a collection of over one hundred styles of greeting cards, and are available in full color. Her media include watercolor, oil, and pencil. For further information, contact Jeanne at *From The Loft*, 618-483-5805, or e-mail dwolff48@frontiernet.net.

The author, whose artwork, originally rendered in oil and India ink, is reproduced on pages 30, 40, and 52.

Abb Vaughn, a former fencing student, whose drawing on page 106 was originally used in the author's promotional fencing pieces.

Mr. Dahlheimer and the author, whose collaborative efforts produced the photograph-turned-artwork of a hydrangea bush in Victoria's garden in Benton Park on page 142.

Jill McPherson, a friend of the author, whose drawing on page 164 was inspired by the author's lyrics in the song *Elle se souvient.*

The cover artwork is a photograph taken by Mr. Dahlheimer at the Chesapeake Eastern Shores during a visit to Au bord de l' eau, the vacation home of the author's daughter, Suzanne Saint Pellicer.

About the Narrator

by Marcel Toussaint

Linda Dahlheimer, who is the architect of the conceptual style for this book, is no stranger to the world of writing. An occasional contributor to the commentary pages of news publications, her more frequent role for a number of years has been editing material for her husband who is a professional writer, author and publisher. She immensely enjoys the other end of the literary spectrum as well, having been an avid reader since early childhood. Stories involving the human condition spanning life from the ancient past well into the distant future have always held special appeal.

A vintage 1890 French Empire style residence, painstakingly restored, has been home since the 1980s, often the gathering place for friends, family, artists, and musicians. She and her husband delight in trying out on guests an endless repertoire of new cuisine, often paired with many hours of lively conversation – conversation that frequently recycles itself into new writing insights and, perhaps, a bit of subsequent editing.

Table of Contents

Foreword 9

Prologue 10

Spring 13

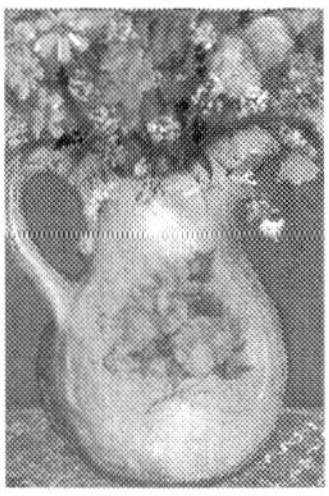

Born on All Saints Day
A Privileged Youth
Leaving Morocco Forever
An Invitation from Uncle Sam
Americanized in Saint Louis
The Next Jacob Mahler
Dueling Master
An Inventor

Summer 99

Courtship and Marriage
Le Papa
Divorce, American Style
A New Beginning
The Victoria Years
The Eastern Shore

Autumn 149

Forays to Balmar Farm
The Bluegrass Connection
The Published Poet
The Poor People of Paris
Benton Park in Bloom

Winter 189

Death – and Rebirth
Sunrise, Sunset
An American in Paris
Life is a Cabaret

Epilogue 205

Photo Album 222

Index of Press Coverage 236

General Index 238

Foreword

By Linda Bernahl Dahlheimer

Sometime in the early nineties, Emil Saint Pellicer began to use "Marcel Toussaint" as his professional name in his published poetry. The author wanted to see if he could be successful in publishing poetry without the recognition that his past achievements had brought him. Because he has generally kept his private life separate from his professional world, many friends and associates initially recognize him by one name and not the other.

The author has written more than one thousand poems. Many of them are also in French and in Spanish. My original intention was to compile his English poems and short stories into a poetry book. But, while cataloging them for easier accessibility, I made a discovery: Many of the poems seemed to represent the various stages of the author's fascinating life. Indeed, through his years of writing poetry, whether intentionally or not, he had created an autobiography.

So began my new vision for the initial poetry project.

This is an autobiography woven together with several components. The author's poems create the foundation for his life story. The narratives written by me are based on years of conversations with the author. The excerpted newspaper accounts enrich his story, and the photos and artwork, created long before this project began, add a visual element.

I may have taken some artistic license with the original intent of some of his poems. Despite the year they were written, I have placed them in a chronological fashion, using the seasons of the year as a metaphor for the various stages of his life.

Toussaint's quotations are interspersed throughout the book to reflect his life stages. Whether the quotations are being used in their original context is something only the author will know for certain.

...ologue

"It is better to write something interesting and die,
than to write nothing, and live.
For this is 'living dead.'"

I Was In Want Of A Past

To think back, when young,
I was in want of a past
that had not yet time to be,
and be left behind.
I wanted something memorable
that I could have done
that would give me some class
beyond the children of my age.
It was important to do well,
excel, competing against myself,
not against them
for I did not want to deny to others
to do the same.

My first life was already long,
well spent, when a cardiac arrest
gave it an end before a recount
of the chapters of my past.
I am not writing to you
from the beyond, a ghost
with a voice from afar.
This is my second life
after the skills of technicians
bombarded with shock blasts
a body at that moment gone
to its last sleep into space.
They succeeded in their efforts,
grabbed me from the bed of clouds
before my entrance into heaven
at the moment that warm bliss
had overtaken me.

My eyes open, flat on my back,
I saw so many white-gowned shadows
staring at me. I could not speak.
I could hear them.
Words did not make any sense,
I only realized I was alive;
something had happened.
Since then, new chapters of life
have taken place, a reprieve
to let me continue for some time
from where I left off, unorganized,
poems, thoughts, quotes, novels in disarray.
There is so much more I want to write
before a new end may become my last.

Marcel Toussaint, 2009

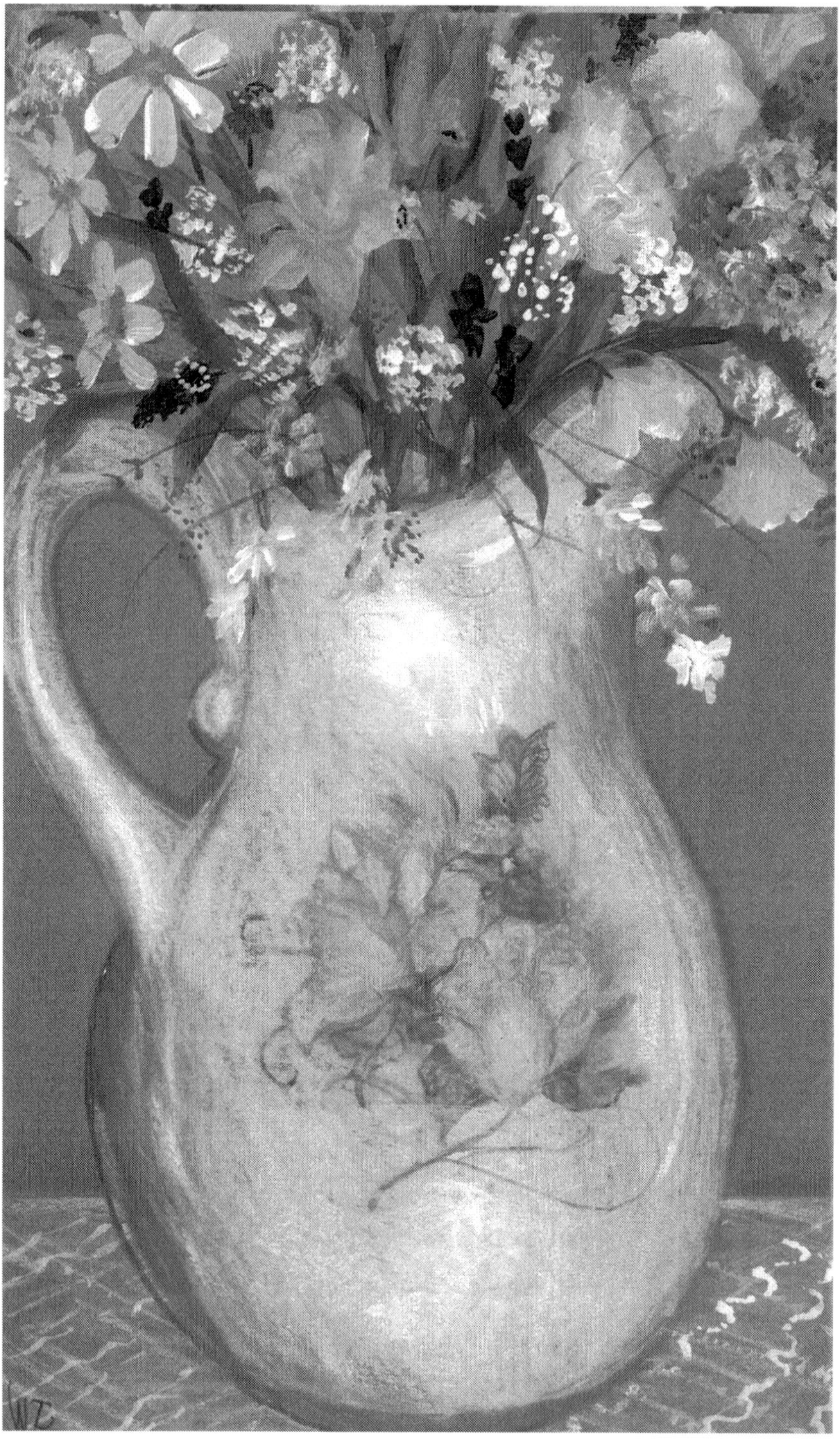

Spring

"Like the seasons, love does not last
but gets renewed in the Spring
or ends in the cold of Winter."

Warmth, Sun And Stars

Opening the door to the outside,
warmth from the night gets in.
Spring started a month early,
buds waiting for a settled battle.

A jealous dark sky lets a few stars shine;
aging winter wants to hold on,
blasting mean gusts of wind
that reach and grip your insides.

The imminent change brings hope
to our awakening yard;
tulips are ready to break through,
slowly testing the air above ground.

The confrontation pursues a last battle.
Winter, relenting its cold command,
springs amiable and convincing
there will be warmth, sun and stars.

It Was The First Day

Like a mature flower soon to blossom,
the zealous singing reached its apogee,
the palpate of the keys in harmony,
the voice, the echo of the love poem.

It was the first day of the Millennium
into the rich hours of the evening
when inspired lovers are still embracing,
kisses pressing into passion's momentum.

The captive audience cheered the finale,
its grandeur not avowing an encore.
The singer's persona perfect rapport
ignited dreams of lasting fantasy.

It was the first day of the Millennium,
starting was a new hopeful adventure
heralded with a vocal signature.
The world...
stopped looking at the pendulum.

November First, Nineteen Hundred and Thirty-Two

Rabat, Morocco

A New Life

"God, in your name let me take command of my life, for no one knows it better."

Birth

Clasping the figurative silver spoon in a tiny fist, Emil Stanley Saint Pellicer made his debut on All Saints Day. The year was nineteen hundred and thirty-two. His mother, an Andalusian señora, and his French-born father had settled in Rabat, Morocco as a result of a transfer by the French Government.

It would be another sixty or so years before Saint Pellicer would expand his persona to include his alter ego, Marcel Toussaint. Many chapters would need to unfold before fate could forge the connection.

Rabat, City For Dreams

When you arrive you adore this place,
wanting to stay for a twenty-year embrace
in the city where the storks like to nest,
where at noon the cactus blooms best.

Forceful white waves of the ocean bellow
against the imposing cliffs overflow,
washing aged ramparts with buds of foam.
In picturesque paradise your eyes roam.

The whitewashed houses overlook the riff,
hugging each other close on top of the cliff,
colors of chalk, sky-blue, stone walls red,
dashes of vegetation, a flowerbed.

Firewood turned charcoal gives its hazy smell.
Soft Arabian music adds to the spell.
Sweet crusty intrigues stuffed with almond paste
let hot tea unleash their delicate taste.

The scent of leather hugs in the Casbah,
Roman ruins nostalgic in the Chehlah,
gardens romantic at the Oudaia,
in the distance, dust clouds a fantasia.

When you arrive you adore the place.
You want to stay for a twenty-year embrace
in the city where the storks like to nest,
where at noon the cactus blooms best.

Rabat, city for dreams retrieval,
Rabat, city for dreams beautiful,
Rabat, city for dreams colorful,
beautiful, colorful, medieval.

Papa

He was so proud to be recognized
as master in his art.
He did not want another title,
although he had to accept
the fact that he was the Chef.
He was skilled in many crafts
for he had the eye and the skilled hands.

Maman's Lump Of Sugar In Rum

For a young child, a lump of sugar in rum,
chest congestion, cough and headache drum.
Maman knew how little she should give;
as the third child, remedy needed no sieve.

I remember the rum, strange bitter taste,
then the softer flavor of lump, sweet-laced.

In a flash, warmth would overtake my chest,
my head forgetting pain so I could rest,
quickly to fall into a deep, long sleep.
Recovery started as morn would creep.

I remember the rum, strange bitter taste,
then the softer flavor of lump, sweet-laced.

Youth

"Life is not just of 'yes' and 'no,'
but of 'maybe.'"

Young and Invincible

His father had expected his only son to direct his interest toward a career as an engineer on the technical side of a radio station. To his dismay, young Saint Pellicer's interests instead gravitated more toward the artistic side of radio. He was far more interested in radio shows, acting, writing, and fine arts. And, had he not been intimidated by his father's fine baritone voice, singing would surely have been added to the budding artist's repertoire.

His was a rich childhood, steeped in many happy memories of Morocco and visits to the family farms. The collection of poems from those days provides clear insight from the perspective of a young boy.

Reading Opens

Reading imparts puzzling old worlds, once ours.
Reading reveals adventure worlds to Mars.
Reading opens reflective worlds of thought.
Reading leaves in our minds these worlds well wrought.

Reading opens.

My Two Most Cherished Toys And Pet

My first most cherished toy was
a spring-wound model car
that ran on a tabletop,
rushing to the edge
making an about-face,
sensing the open void
to run to another edge,
never, ever falling to the floor.

My second most cherished toy was
a small boat painted in bright colors
with people at port holes
looking out to the Bath Sea
in my water-filled bathtub.

.

The boat had a firing chamber
where a small candle was placed
lit to warm up a reservoir
with two tubing
extending to the back
to propel the boat
around the walls
of this improvised
confining sea.

My pet was a white mouse
with red eyes,
active and fast
with the hope to run away
from the confines of its small cage.

In time, the car needed repairs;
it was misplaced or lost.
Next, the boat required repairs
to the leaking reservoir;
it could not be found.

Then, in time, the white mouse
was last seen
as Maman took her
to the bathroom,
and we heard a big flush.

I cried, wanting her back,
but Maman was in charge.
She loved her three children,
but would not raise a mouse.

Maman could not see why
one keeps broken toys.
Quietly, she removed them from sight.
She may have had something to do
with their disappearance,
an act she did without a second thought.

But my memories cannot be discarded.
They are vivid, full of smiles and joy,
recalling the grand moments
of a young boy with toys
from Christmases past.

The School Years

"In school I was taught to speak in syllables,
but I was born before the telegraph."

Could This Last All Year?

The smell of the lacquer on the pencils
in October is new.
Sharpened at the blade the wood unrolled
like rings as it grew.
A fine lead powder lands on the desk
from where the wind blew.

The hardbound books are of paper,
bleached, written in dark ink.
To the touch, quality; to the eyes, a pleasure.
Writings to make us think
with the knowledge we now read
as fast as a blink.

The satchel is of fine Moroccan leather,
fragrant and new.
The buckle shiny with chrome,
craftsmanship from a crew.
The pelt of a grazing cow
who gave her last "Moo!"

After a long summer, so much, too much,
forming a link;
teachers, books, pencils, faces unknown.
A girl at whom I wink,
long hair, tresses in a ponytail
that I will dip into ink.

Could this last all year?

JW

The First Crush Of My Life

In class I would turn to steal a quick look
to see her there, studious, reading her book.
Weary, the teacher could tell me to move.
Yes, even when she had nothing to prove.

I ran to school to catch up with her walk
Yet, when at her side, I could not even talk!
Of life there was lots that she could teach me.
She was taller, older. It just had to be.

She had an easy smile, one of great joy.
I acted so shy – she would soon know my ploy.
With a scorching burn soon taking me over,
I was hoping, with her, to count leaves of clover.

To reach her house I often changed my route.
I rode with the hope she would quickly come out.
With nothing to say, and a thrill through my spine,
should, with a smile, her eyes look into mine.

Why so very young did I feel this way?
Not knowing, in time, it could lead to play.
She would not notice me in my springtime
and, at nine, could not share in a lifetime.

The first crush of my life
I thought of, all the time.

The Grade School Bully

With a disturbed glare, his mind a whole lump,
he was a taller kid, yet built like a stump.
On shoulders sat a head too large for his size;
was there anything behind those dark eyes?

The grade school bully was compulsive,
aggressive, destructive, vindictive.

His body language was plainly combative.
When he crossed my eyes with his negative,
a surge of anger flowed onto his face.
His chest gasping, restraint showed no trace.

Strong, he geared up his forces for aggress,
leaned, launched himself forward with duress.
Small and fast, I moved away from his path,
avoiding his surprise attacks, and his wrath.

Spying from his house, he could see and rule
if I was walking the last stretch to school.
Revising his tactics, he set to sneak,
rushing behind me, sure I would freak.

Gifted with a clear wide-angle vision,
the corner of my eye spotted his action.
He lifted his leg for a vicious kick.
Duping him, I remained without panic.

I curved, lifted my right hand and then hooked
his raised left ankle. Then I quickly ducked
to flip him sideways, and flat to the ground.
To school I then ran, as fast as a hound.

I resolved to get around with the bike.
This would deter the bully's surprise hike.
As he walked along the sidewalk, as the fool,
safely, I rode the whole stretch to the school.

Childhood Mystique

Characters, settings originative,
all writings must be imaginative.
Brush strokes are used in various descriptions
while boldly painting for great impressions.

Perfecting and lost in such a technique,
we recreate our own childhood mystique
What we were once, we recognize no more.
After all, who wants to remain a bore?

The Teenage Years

"We do not give credit to sixteen year olds
for the good things they do
and the bad things they look to get into."

You Wake Up Thirteen

Suddenly today, you wake up thirteen,
the same as yesterday but now a teen.
You will feel different starting tomorrow.
Gradually you will want to overthrow
the authority you find pure nonsense,
and calm the love that will remain intense.

Remember this happy birthday.

As the early morn fades into high noon
your growing up comes for us much too soon.
Yes, let us hold you in our arms once more
before, to new ventures you cry out, "fore!"
You are now thirteen and losing your dimple,
replaced, on your brow, with the dreaded pimple!

Happy, With A Tear In My Eye

I recall growing up curious ,
wanting to know all I could,
going to the best schools,
sheltered from danger, financially secure
in a civilization that was not mine.

I loved the sun and the Moorish ruins,
the old Roman bath in the Chellah,
the harsh breaking waves against the rocks.
Perched high,I lingered into the past
with dreams of pirates and their frigates.

How could they come and dock?
They must have anchored in the estuary,
then reached the short beach by small boats.
They would ransack the whitewashed village
that clung on the steep, forbidding cliffs.

Cannons awaiting behind the fortress walls
pointed at any suspicious arrival.
Some cannon balls still on the ground
too heavy for anyone to lift and take
remained there within the red clay enclave.

I climbed the Hassan Tower many a time,
walking up the ramp and examining the
chambers with open windows to wind and rain.
The winters were damp, sometimes grey;
the summers hot, but cool in the tower's draft.

From the top I saw Rabat, its sister city Salé,
the dividing Bou Regreg mostly with shallow waters,
trees here and there but not enough,
a few cacti that found the most arid places,
the waterman walking with his gourd and a shining cup.

During that time my ancestors in Spain,
my ancestors in France, were bathed with the arts,
the literature, the music of a great past
that I wanted to savor better, not just on radio.
In this Mediterranean world, who was I?

The wars, the distance, the governments
restricted what would have been normal.
In my formative years they deprived me
of all that I needed to know to be the real me
in a world in disarray with dictators and wars.

I recall the wonders of my surrounds
warm and safe, interesting and quiet.
These were wonderful years, with music
that got into my mind to never forget,
a mint tea that lifted my spirits when sad.

But now, at the conclusion of my life,
I see how I missed my own roots.
There, blatant, is the fact
that all would have been different,
different in a way I will never know.

I fondly reminisce my youth, the way it was
and the way it was not.
Nothing I would change,
happy, with a tear in my eye.

England and Paris

"Good deportment is a passport
to travel into society at any level."

Fourteen In A Foreign Land

So long were dull days washed by a fine rain,
cold sun rays, a routine sun without smiles
retreating guilty in the British Isles
clouds bringing no joy but visual strain.

With only a tandem for getting around,
alone, feeling absurd riding, face burning,
pedaling in front, back pedals turning,
my invisible passenger not making a sound.

Late Summer, I waited for five o'clock
for that was when the fireplace got lighted.
If sooner, the landlady was sighted,
out checking for smoke from chimney. Oh, shock!

Knock on door: "My dear, your logs are firing.
It is not yet time to burn up the fuel.
For once, I wish you would respect the rule!
Yet, of Continentals, it is too much for asking."

Most times I was cold, beneath skies of grey;
wearing two sweaters did not help my plight.
Gloomy sitting room alit by dim gaslight,
the weak glow letting me read to pass the day.

Sunday to the Commons, a patch of grass,
looking for retreat under covered niche,
umbrella ready for a weather glitch,
in public square, growing weeds with class.

We took sandwiches, coffee, on a hike
for a pleasant foray from the landlady's drone.
Would she dare to tail along, I would then groan!
Islanders search for the dull life they like.

Why be unfriendly to the foreign import,
visitor taking a European detour?
They can hold to their dull days quite secure.
No right mind would capture them for export.

Seeking to improve upon his English, the teenager's fourteenth year marked a solo journey to England where he lived with his sister, Josephine, and her English husband, Derek Carter.

Saint Pellicer had been a child when Derek and Josie first met at an international dance in Rabat. Derek, during his stay in Rabat as an enlisted man with the Royal Air Force, became young Saint Pellicer's first English tutor. Following their wedding in Rabat, the Carters lived in England and Pakistan before eventually settling in the United States. Derek was a professor of Aeronautical Engineering at Parks College of Saint Louis University for many years.

Saint Pellicer's return trip to Morocco three months later included a stopover in Paris. There, a French couple at the airport had seen the emotional goodbyes between the teenager and his English family, and had noticed he looked disoriented and lost. They approached him and offered their assistance. The friendly exchange led to an opportunity for a sightseeing trip around Paris, including the top of the Eiffel Tower, the terrace high above the Arc de Triomphe, and a show at the famous Moulin Rouge.

All too soon it was time to return to the airport for the flight to Casablanca and, for the second time in a day, he would bid farewell, this time to his new friends. The friendship would continue by way of correspondence for some years.

Recent painting by Jeanne Wolff, based on early photograph of Spanish composer, Jose Padilla, great-uncle of Emil Saint Pellicer.

Famous Great-Uncle

Saint Pellicer would in time appreciate that the Moulin Rouge had been a popular venue in the twenties and thirties for the music of his famous relative, Jose Padilla. Padilla, whose music was used in over three hundred films, was the uncle of Saint Pellicer's mother.

The following information was provided by Christopher Webber on zarzuela.net:

> Padilla had trained at the Madrid conservatory and in Italy, before rapidly immersing himself in Madrid theatre life.
>
> While living in Paris, he wrote the scores for two opérettes, *Pépète* and *Symphonie Portugaise.* Many of his songs were incorporated in revues at the Moulin Rouge. *El relicario* and *Valencia,* which has become a sort of Spanish national anthem, brought him international celebrity.
>
> *My Spanish Rose* later appeared in Jerome Kern's score for the Broadway musical, *The Night Boat.* Padilla wrote music for Mistinguett, Maurice Chevalier, Josephine Baker, and many more. One of his pieces, *La violetera,* is included in the famous silent film, *City Lights.*
>
> Despite his success abroad, Padilla continued to write for the Spanish stage. He died in Madrid in 1960.

Many years later Saint Pellicer would become acquainted with Alois Broeke, from the Netherlands, a well-known writer on Latin and mechanical music. In 2004, Broeke wrote a well-received article on Jose Padilla, which was published in *Het Pierement,* the quarterly magazine for fans of mechanical organs.

Mr. Broeke specializes in Cuban and Argentinean music, especially the tango, and automatic playing instruments. Saint Pellicer and Broeke remained in contact as the article was being written and published. They continue to correspond across the continents.

I Imagined The Moulin Rouge

In front of the imposing Windmill and its red
we are in line to enter.
I discern all, the simplest details,
the public, the posters, the curtains,
the lively colors, red, ochre and brass.
I want to return to the past,
the grandiose days and nights
of our ancestors at venues, at concerts.

I imagined the Moulin Rouge of those times,
the intoxicating music,
the anticipation of the entry on stage
of beautifully slender, elegant girls,
parading themselves in mini costumes,
their large feathered fans hiding
just as soon to unveil
their exciting attributes.

I imagined Mistinguett singing
Ça C'est Paris to the music
of my great-uncle
José Padilla Sanchez,
Spanish composer,
in his glory years, in the twenties and thirties,
and of his famous Paso Doble, Valencia,
and the unforgettable El Rélicario.

I imagined Paris, City of Lights,
cheerful, sparkling and feasting;
the cars shiny, standing in line,
their drivers in uniforms,
their occupants in white tie and evening dress,
slowly depositing the guests
under the marquee's luminance
of the main door.

Once inside, well placed,
after a flute of champagne,
a toast to the memory of José,
the orchestra played engaging refrains.
With Almarie, my daughter, I danced a Cha Cha,
then a Swing with Linda
on the dance floor next to the platform, where Mistinguett
sang, to the music of my great-uncle.

It was a moment of emotions
created by the past and the present,
a memorable bringing together.
I felt close to my present family
with a link to the one of times past.
I imagined my great-uncle composing new melodies
for my lyrics, giving to them liveliness.

I imagined.

Back to Morocco

After his return from England, the young student continued to immerse himself in his studies, and prepare himself for life's challenges outside of the academic world. Because of his interest in literature and theatre, he enrolled in the Art Dramatique class at the Conservatoire and performed in classical French plays on stage. From there he applied at Radio-Maroc and was accepted as a teenage actor in the Emission Enfantine and Variety show under the direction of producer-director Marise Valli.

Saint Pellicer lived in a world of languages, speaking French with his father and Spanish with his mother. His first exposure to English occurred in 1943 with the landing of the troops in North Africa. English became part of the dinners for American and English soldiers, guests at the home of his parents.

Saint Pellicer decided to take English as his first foreign language at the College des Orangers in Rabat. An honor student in English, he received the coveted First Prize for English for six straight years. This distinction would eventually earn him a role as interpreter.

Water Complex, Plain

There, a young man writing,
flipping pages, from the table across,
throwing his gaze over my shoulders,
to water complex without the fountain.

What he was seeing was rather bland.
But the skill of a pen
can change what is blank,
bring in emotions,
ferment what it may, detect secrets,
reveal the forgotten obvious
we choose to ignore conscious.

He could not see the same tableau,
the fountain virile piercing high in flight.
I wondered what he would have written,
whatever would be in the present tense,
for the past he was not there to grasp
the lingering splashes recall of events.

Reminder of me at a younger age
in French walking shorts,
favorite striped shirt of blue,
body slender of very young years
spent way too fast, never meant to last;
for it is only now the past means so much,
blind energy uneven, weakened.

There, a young man leaving,
closing his pages, from the table across;
gone his gaze over my shoulders,
holding memories of water complex, plain.

A Different Way

As a boy I wanted to do as other boys do,
I thought.
It meant to be tough, rough, boisterous, mean.
It was not me.
I wanted to be physical and punch the other guy.
I was not built for that, and lost many a fight.
I felt that I had to lie, for it was the way out.
It was not.

To revenge myself was primary.
A mistake it was.
There was passion in it,
it seemed.
It was anger, very destructive.

One thing was obvious.
I had a vicious, clever repartee
that was often rewarded with a black eye.
And it did not disappear overnight.

Soon I realized I was not that guy.
I analyzed my emotions.
I had to curb my language,
as it got me into fights.
I had to renounce revenge;
it got me into fights.

Being jealous was a problem.
It got me nowhere.
It tightened my insides.
It made me feel bad.

It was time to remodel my personality.
It was hard.

A Colorful Blend of Family and Culture

As a youth, Saint Pellicer's life revolved around a rich blend of cultures. From his mother came the Spanish influence. His father, French. Living in Morocco provided a third culture – Arabic.

My Cousin From Casablanca

Of independence she was at the age,
free to think, free to act, it would well last.
Knowing how to live, each day a new page
in the vibrant city pictured in my past.
She was my cousin from Casablanca.

I admired her meticulous presence,
her beauty enhanced by her make-up, light,
a warm perfume of the lightest essence.
Inherited with grace were her eyes, bright.
She was my cousin from Casablanca.

Elegant, she walked; you noticed her pace.
She designed hats, wore them in high fashion.
Dressed with the latest, highest heels in place,
a smile, a kind word was her real passion.
She was my cousin from Casablanca.

She had reached the years of discovery
a few years ahead, too distant for me,
keeping to herself all the mystery
in a city alive bathed by the sea.
She was my cousin from Casablanca.

Invited To Weddings, Initiation

Invited to weddings, initiation
to Islam at young boy's circumcision.
During these events we would sit
at low, round tables of brass, candlelit,
geometric designs grooved into the top
by artful hands at the artisan shop.
Our hosts wearing their best were so festive;
in the afternoon, their calm was most restive.

The furnishings simple and adequate,
a style that local traditions mandate.
The low built-in couches had no soft springs,
were low wooden boxes or pine casings
covered with assorted blankets, woven by hand,
wool flaming red, brilliant blue, deep green, sand,
with a contrasting Arabesque design,
often natural white and fringed outline.

Stuffed firm with crushed newspaper, no feather,
poufs of luxurious Moroccan leather
with pleasant smell of recently tanned pelts;
strips of contrasting leather rose like welts
in and out of the side, on top of each pouf.
This was a room where nothing was fireproof.
With knees cracking, we used the low hassocks,
for all seating was on square or round blocks.

We sat with the proud head of the household
with only one woman by the threshold.
Her self-effacing manner seeming quite nettle,
she came in to bring the boiling kettle –
its new copper bottom had turned red hot.
Water was poured slowly into the teapot.
First, from just above, the pouring was done,
then, with an up-down action hard to clone.

Very same style was used to fill our glass;
custom never called for use of a tasse.
Flowing water in rhythm, splashing sound,
I watched the ritual, my eyes astound.
Body immobile on a small red pouf,
escaping steam upward onto the roof.
Done with accuracy, there was no spilling,
each glass getting the same even filling.

Such intense heat released the rich flavor
of green tea, fresh mint leaves into a vapor,
an aroma to bathe your taste buds, raise
passion, firing your vigor to a blaze.
Sugar comes in a foot cone-shaped column
with the look of a white candle, so solemn.
The host breaks with ease each uneven chunk,
striking against a stone with a very sharp clunk.

Water so very hot, tea needs less steep.
Even the thin glass sides could not weep.
Hold your glass by the rim and bottom edge;
being careful becomes a much-needed pledge.
The scalding tea barely touching your lips,
draw slowly this nectar, and pause between sips.
Our host with gusto makes a sipping sound,
his eyes almost closed, looking toward ground.

In a different hut, the women have their feast,
on their own, and not bothered in the least.
Moresque formality, many beaux gestes,
all men in main hut, even women guests.
An exception between two peoples' mores,
both sides content with no dissenting roars.
The children were not seen in the old way.
This was an adult affair, and not for young play.

Couscous a la Marocaine

At home maman had the maid do couscous
from scratch on a grey marble table; loose
semolina spread out over fine cloth,
the end process to be as light as froth,
by circling damp hands creating clusters
with water droplets in controlled thrusters.
When enough was prepared, then let to dry,
hungry, impatient, I came in to spy.

The maid, donned in her native dress,
gave a country flair to the cooking process.
She had been with us since we came from town.
She was always happy, her spirits never down.
Maman was generous. She wanted Fatima
to live well and healthy, as she said "supra."
Once a year we were asked to her home,
an honor, near a white Marabou dome.

Special double cooker filled casserole,
bottom with vegetables caracole,
almonds, sometimes raisins, mutton or lamb,
chicken, some zucchini added in jam.
Water from the well to create a stew,
soaked in heavy broth, a heavenly brew.
The steam piercing couscous up through strainer,
a linen wrapped on seam above boiler.

We served couscous true a la Marocaine.
Even with old friends we would entertain
in a bright glazed terra cotta round dish,
anxious to save the V bone for a wish.
Mound of couscous, spicy broth, vegetables abound,
in a circle, saffron-flavored, meat crowned.

The Señora From Spain

The body arched, Andalusian mold,
a dark dress hugging, a fan unfold,
a capricious hand lifting a curl deep brown,
a haughty chignon circles a rose crown.

Fine brows arched over vivacious eyes
sunk in a tanned and proud face, a prize.
Her lips sanguine, aristocratic, refined,
a perfect nose, a pretty chin well defined.

Sharp high heels flatter her elongated legs.
Her fine yet disturbing silhouette begs
to be admired, recognized, her pose blatant,
a woman wanting love, her passion vibrant.

I gaze my eyes on this painting, awesome
who wakes up in me love's wisdom.
My blood rushing in every vein curve,
quieting wise constraints of chivalrous verve.

Close, real close, her perfume assaults;
tempting, her engaging smile exalts;
her eyes raised, saying, "Don't stand and be;
here I am, to love; kiss me."

My hands capture her shoulders slowly,
wanting to hold this passion fiery,
surfaces a stare asking for a kiss;
defeated, my lips touch hers with bliss.

As if lost, she lodges statuesque
into my arms surround, epic Romanesque
my craving body inflamed with love.
For we are one, fitted as a glove.

The señora from Spain, a fan unfold,
a haughty chignon, a tanned face bold.
The señora from Spain.

Where We Dream The Best

It is in Spain that we dream the best,
where we find affectionate lovers,
where the noon sun forces you to retire in the shade
'til the evening, and the sound of the castanets.

Forced in the corridor is an air current;
the floor tiles, moist, do chill the place.
We enjoy the cool air and overwhelming heat
in the country where all stops, even the dancers.

The heavy shutters are closed, fighting the sun.
Only in Spain do we see that happen.
We dream of evenings, we dream of brunettes
dressed in blazing colors, in hand, castanets.

Once the torrid sun is put to bed and forgotten,
quickly the still of the day disappears.
The shutters open, life blossoms
like a flower that challenges boredom.

The Sevillanas do their pirouettes,
striking their heels under the stars
on the paved streets in melodious echoes,
unfolding the want of the desirous eyes.

Flamencos go beyond midnight,
to the lovers that the frenzy pursue;
passion, their blood boils, persevered,
and their dreams become realities.

It is in Spain that we succumb to love.
It is in Spain that we feel victorious.
It is in Spain that we dream the best.

By The Mediterranean Sea

The sun of the Midi is warming.
I am on the balcony, a landscape striking.
Over roofs and terraces, in the distance,
is the Mediterranean reflecting surface.

A breeze caresses the foliage
that moves under its passing breath.
Stripes of grey and white clouds
light themselves in the sky, in the foreground.

The song of the birds is frivolous,
in the skies nothing does fly.
They know it will get very hot;
they rest in the shade, close to the water.

The view of roads held in silence;
the cars roll in hushed rhythm.
We see no one walking the paths.
A noisy helicopter ruins the moment.

My fingers run on the keyboard.
I write without the need of paper.
The screen is difficult to read.
This could be even worse.

A canopy protects me from the sun;
but new rays awaken,
slip through to reach up to me
and you, if you were here.

How marvelous to have so much light
far from the grey of the forgotten North.
One wants to stretch out under the sky.

Immersed in the Arts

"Creativity seldom relies on the past."

Leave Your Mark

Young adult, time has come to leave your mark.
It is best to be remembered with a spark.
Secure, ready to climb life's skyscraper,
your name proudly headlining fine notepaper.

Your writings must make of words a sculpture
with your name printed as your signature.
How well you will be remembered, not dead,
for it is now the time to tell, you are well bred.

Leave Your Mark!

Saint Pellicer's young years are described in a 1960 *Saint Louis Globe-Democrat* article:

> "As a teenager, he performed over Radio-Maroc with fourteen other actors for two years. The group did two shows a week, one drama, and the other variety. Dancing came naturally, too, from his student years at the Conservatoire de Musique, where all of the arts were taught except painting."

It was during this time that a mishap changed his life forever.

Life Is Of Interruptions

Life is of interruptions
We start and stop, restart,
all over again.

The spontaneity lost
may not be there ever,
ever again.

But we can have another try.
Another and another,
without an end.

Smartly, we cope with delays,
we persist and persist.
We have learned to bend.

A Life-Altering Experience

"To look is not to see."

While on his way to his sister Odette's wedding, the bus in which he was riding was broadsided by a large truck. He missed the wedding and ended up in a clinic in Casablanca. After a week of hospitalization, the chief doctor noted that the compound fracture of Saint Pellicer's left leg had several blackened areas. Dr. Conte quickly pulled out a sizable chunk of gangrenous material from the wound and told the frightened teenager that he would need to undergo an amputation above the ankle to stop the spread of gangrene.

At this revelation, young Saint Pellicer bolted upright on the examining table and emphatically declared there would be no surgery. At age nineteen he had no intention of losing any part of his leg. When Dr. Conte responded that the defiant teenager would then have to undergo the only procedure possible to rid his body of gangrene, the relieved young man immediately agreed to the treatment. At that moment he had no idea what the "treatment" entailed.

Just then, a tray bearing gauze and medical utensils was brought in. Two nurses and a massive orderly held the anxious patient to the operating table. Using great care, Dr. Conte proceeded to scrape the flesh wounds down to the bone, all the while sterilizing with rubbing alcohol. Through clenched teeth in a futile attempt to lessen the agony, Saint Pellicer screamed endlessly. There was good reason to feel tormented – no painkiller had been administered.

At last the session ended, and the strong grips that had held him down were relaxed. He felt enormous relief and a sense of restored comfort. And then the young patient was informed that the treatment was far from over. There would be repeat sessions twice a day – for a month.

The experience had demonstrated a tenacity for keeping his body intact, and would prepare him for a new direction and challenges.

Bionic Dennis

Soon you will be better than brand new,
and conceal that your hip holds by a screw.

With vigor moving well on a new joint,
you will continue making it a point.

In sports, your forte is playing tennis.
You will be known as "Bionic Dennis!"

An Offer He Would Refuse

*"Trying to be perfect can ruin one's life.
What or whose standards should perfection use?
Sincerely doing the best one possibly can
is the right course."*

Following his recovery, Saint Pellicer was once again reminded that his father had not given up on the dream for his only son to be an engineer. If he stayed at home, he was informed, and furthered his studies to become an engineer, he would immediately get a new American car.

It was apparent that he needed to make some decisions with regard to his future. Clearly he would never be able to pursue his dreams if he stayed at home, dictated by his father's influence.

Although unhappy to leave his acting at the radio station, Saint Pellicer accepted a position in Sidi Slimane, Morocco, first as a timekeeper interpreter, and then as a cost accountant interpreter. Sidi Slimane was situated at the edge of the desert. Weather conditions were often torrid, and the job required living in tents.

As the 1960 story in the *Saint Louis Globe–Democrat* continued,

> "At 19, he went to Sidi Slimane, Morocco, where he worked for two American companies, Atlas Constructors and the United States Air Force base. For a Frenchman able to speak English, that led naturally to a job with U.S.A.F. as interpreter."

Eventually he decided to leave for the United States. There he would begin a new life. His English professor, Madame Marambaud, had suggested the States rather than England, noting that the Americans would be more receptive to his style of writing than the English.

His childhood years spent, he said goodbye to his beloved Morocco. Saint Pellicer recalls how his mother, at the last moment, wept and pleaded for him to change his mind and stay at home in Rabat. Her passionate appeals had once worked with his older sister. This time, however difficult, the young man knew he must fulfill his destiny, and would not be swayed.

Leaving Morocco Forever

"No people can accept or allow
the taking of its soil."

In The Sadness Of Leaving

In the sadness of leaving our birth country,
one keeps the most beautiful memories
the happiest of the unfolded days
in what becomes in the present - the past.

In the country that one never can forget,
that never stops to marvel,
one leaves behind a trail of regrets,
moments of discreet weaknesses.

It is there that our youth evolved,
where our need to grow we pressed
with an impatient inducement
like the refrains of engaging songs.

To this country one always returns
with very short hellos
or long memory reminders
that re-sketch what stood for glory.

One promises often a return
but it becomes a set of detours;
for our new country keeps us jealous,
in place, grounded by a nail.

From Casablanca to Saint Louis

Saint Pellicer arrived in Saint Louis on Independence Day. It was the year of his twenty-first birthday. During his time in Saint Louis, he lived with his sister, Odette, and her husband, William Comer.

Odette had been the secretary of a commander at the U.S. Naval Base at Port Lyautey in Kenitra, Morocco when she met her husband who was stationed at Port Lyautey. They were married there, and eventually moved to the United States.

William's father, Joseph Comer, a plant superintendent at Woodward and Tiernan Printing Company in Saint Louis, filed the sponsorship papers for Saint Pellicer's immigration to the United States. Each year, to show his appreciation, Saint Pellicer would bring Joseph Comer and his wife a bottle of champagne on the anniversary of his arrival.

The young immigrant would soon discover that his initial stay in Saint Louis would be brief.

Nothing Lasts Forever

When I came I felt as an intruder.
I gave the wrong impression of a snob,
for I had lived in my father's world,
a millionaire.
To accumulate money, bills,
was never my game.
I was able to do as I pleased.
Learning many skills
to build a profession
for retirement
was never on my mind.
But nothing lasts forever.

The Fourth

What a calm lazy day!
May this day be a happy birthday
of a nation
who has given so much to the world
and has a lot more to give
in these troubled times.

This is the day that I celebrate
my American life
with gratitude.
May the word of God remain
in its most important documents and hymns.

Anyone who does not agree
should be given the choice
to leave.

Military Life

"When will the authorities learn that they are Public Servants?"

He was drafted into the United States Army within eight months. Foreigners are often inducted into the Armed Forces before becoming United States citizens.

Fort Leonard Wood Basic Training

"You said, 'Hey, you!'
I could not respond.
It is not my name."

His stint in the U.S. Army began with a few days at "Little Korea," as Fort Leonard Wood was called. Early memories include the dusty grounds and roads, and the ill-kept barracks. He wondered why he was there. Unaccustomed to such orders as, "Do as I say," and, "Do not ask questions," the young soldier learned quickly that keeping a low profile was best.

Yes, Sir!

Camouflaged behind a gas mask
I carried a canteen, a duffel bag,
a rolled sack, M1 strapped on shoulder, a mag,
head crushed, ears lost into a military cask.

Came a brawny sergeant making little sense.
I would have liked to fence!

At reveille shaken to a fanfare,
running place to place in baggy underwear,
fatigues rubbing my skin bare,
boots of leather dry, I needed a wheelchair.

"Fall in! Fall out! Ten-shun! At ease!"
Basic, basic language, nonsense a breeze.

Before dawn, buttoning pants to sprint,
my heart wild losing a beat,
out of breath overcome by heat,
fell down ravine and left footprint.

Came a brawny sergeant shouting, "On the double!"
We all knew it meant trouble.

"Yes, Sir!" to the sergeant from hell
who could not say my name,
for cleaning pots and pans I blame,
who I wanted sent back to hell.

"Fall in! Fall out! Ten-shun! At ease!"
Basic, basic language, nonsense a breeze.

Fort Carson Field Training

Soon after, orders came to report to Fort Carson, Colorado. Military training was interesting at times. The directives of the sergeants in charge of the troops were not easy to ignore, and often seemed illogical.

After many lengthy runs before daybreak at increasingly fast paces, Saint Pellicer began to suffer from shortness of breath and near fainting. Reducing his run to a walk, he realized that he could not continue. He began noticing that each morning, a few soldiers would run down the hills and direct themselves to a barracks in the dark of the camp. One day he followed, and came upon a dispensary unit. Curious, he entered, and found himself among fellow companions of misfortune.

During a physical, the doctor noticed the damaged leg, and a body not conditioned for hard labor and stress. He recommended that Saint Pellicer apply for a medical release from the Army that would take a few weeks to process.

The suggestion worried the young soldier. Such a release seemed to him degrading. The term itself was ambivalent. He felt that a medical discharge would have a negative impact on employment opportunities back in Missouri.

Added to these concerns was the issue of citizenship, which was of great importance to Saint Pellicer. A legal officer had said that an immigrant in the services was eligible for citizenship after three months. This meant he would need to stay in the service for two years. There just was no alternative but to refuse such a discharge.

The dispensary provided the determined soldier a medical slip, advising him to never let it out of his hands. Without the slip, Saint Pellicer would have to do what was medically restricted. Sergeants were notorious about asking for a slip, and not returning it.

So ended his field training with the troops. Boots were returned to the quartermaster and replaced with low quarter shoes.

Veterans At Christmas

Special ornaments are on the Christmas tree,
remembering our veterans with glee,
with no exceptions – World War I and II,
then Korea, Vietnam, Desert Storm, too.
Far back to the Civil War conciliates,
soldiers of the North and confederates,
Mexican and any forgotten war.
Held in sorrow, pride, hope in treetop star.
A new beginning: The Infant is born.
Let's celebrate our veterans, and not mourn.

Service to the Officers

"Brass must be shined every day
to look like gold."

Somehow his designation was passed along through the ranks and, before long, Saint Pellicer found himself in a new assignment. He was designated by the sergeant in charge of the mess hall to serve the officers their three meals each day, tableside.

Breakfast was the most difficult for the young Frenchman with a British accent not accustomed to everyday "American" English. His feet together and with a short bow, he would approach an officer and say, "Good morning, sir, what would you like for breakfast?" This sophistication was too much for some of the officers, who would wonder where this recruit had learned such odd behavior. Others were delighted with his style.

Saint Pellicer quickly realized that at times he needed to confer with the cooks on the other side of the serving table when taking breakfast orders. He had never come across expressions such as *sunny-side up* and *over easy* in any of the English manuals he had studied in his six years in foreign languages.

When the time came for him to be transferred again, the officers wanted to keep the aristocratic European at the mess hall. They had come to enjoy the touch of class he served up with their meals. Indeed the orders were actually stopped – but only for a brief time. After a short break in Saint Louis, Saint Pellicer, in his prized Nash Ambassador, set out for the quartermaster school in Fort Lee, Virginia.

Fort Lee
Back to School

The tone of training was different at Fort Lee. For one thing, there was no harassment from sergeants. It was more of a school with lectures and tests related to the quartermaster fields. The marching to and from the classrooms was in platoon formation, the long walk from the barracks pleasant. There was a certain pleasure in marching in formation when everyone was in step with the rhythm of motion.

It seemed that every single day was a repeat of the preceding. Life here was set and was similar to community living. Scheduled inspections by the officers were conducted in a repeating cycle. To ther dismay, all soldiers, in and out of uniform, regularly marched together. One day, when a colonel was scheduled to review the troops, the order went out that those not in complete uniform would henceforth walk in a little group behind the troop formation. Uniformity had won out.

This dictum included, of course, Saint Pellicer, out of uniform, and limping along in low quarters. The little group of misfits was no doubt an eyesore to the military purists obsessed with uniformity. Saint Pellicer and his colleagues were now segregated from those in full uniform, walking on their own through the fields between the barracks and the school.

Saint Pellicer followed those orders – for a while. But the need to move rapidly just behind the platoons was taxing. And he felt it damaged his foot and leg. He soon found a way to resolve the problem by driving his car to the classroom – from a safe distance behind.

Soldiers Will Be … Soldiers

Graduation day came. The day before departure, the soldiers were given time off and a pass to go off base, and expected to return by midnight. Saint Pellicer observed that, upon graduation, the once well-behaved students who had always obeyed orders now suddenly became unruly and disruptive. Even as he was preparing for his pass, the pranksters were already setting up traps for unsuspecting soldiers returning late that night.

Wary, he packed his duffel bag, made his bed and waited for darkness to set in before he moved to his Nash, which had been parked in a remote area. Once inside the car, he lowered the passenger seat, and surreptitiously settled into his blanket for a night's sleep.

The following day Saint Pellicer awakened before dawn, and quietly returned to the barracks with his duffel bag. What he found did not surprise him. Strings had been tied between beds at the entrance with the hope that returning and inebriated soldiers would end up tripping on the strings. Some belongings were moved to different beds creating confusion once it was time to find the right place.

The ever-vigilant Saint Pellicer had avoided the booby traps. His companions asked him where he had been, as they had been looking for him the night before. Not surprisingly, their question was left unanswered.

After a while, new orders arrived. Following another stopover in Saint Louis, the next destination would be Fort McPherson in Atlanta, Georgia.

Vibrant Opportunist

Coming in a maroon car
was Captain Bard.
Ribbons on his coat of various colors,
cap on a tilt favoring his right,
military attack is visual sight.

Hands on window sill
with big grin was Captain Bard,
words forming, lips apart.
No sounds,
a crowd too far away
to want his thoughts.

Clapping of hands, dust blowing,
sun hot, spirits high for party
to start at night.
Captain tango will drag right foot
on floor
with twist of torso
as Brazil's drums hit.

Vibrant opportunist
is Captain Bard.

Fort McPherson Military Police

According to a 1960 story in the former *St. Louis Globe-Democrat*:

> "As is wont of special service officers, they discovered Saint Pellicer could dance superbly and put him to work in service club ballrooms. In Atlanta, he won first prize in the waltz."

Alas, in Atlanta there was little time for waltzing. Saint Pellicer reported to the Third Army Headquarters where he was assigned to the Military Police as a personal property clerk in the offices of the stockade. A diminutive soldier in full police uniform, he was glad not to have to carry a gun.

The duty was simple: As the incoming prisoners, flanked by two guards, appeared at his door window, he listed all of their belongings, safeguarded in sealed envelopes bearing signatures on the flap, and put into a safe. This included watches, pens, and other personal items found in their pockets. Money was counted and a receipt given for future release. Many complained that valuables were not returned to them during the initial frisking. Here, at the personal property office, only what was actually brought in could be listed.

The guards would ask Saint Pellicer to go with them to the prison to see what it was like. Suspicious of their motivations, he never accepted the invitation. He was skeptical of possible mischief. In time, he sensed that his seriousness and application to his duties were unsettling to the guards and other clerks.

The awkward relationship may have contributed to the next problem. He had been assigned to see that all the beds in the eight-man dormitory he slept in were made up to regulation. Inexplicably, Saint Pellicer could not get himself to properly make the beds of others. It was difficult enough that his bed be made correctly. To see about the other beds was something he just could not do. As a result, every day he was receiving bad points for the poorly-made beds. Because of the uncomfortable relationship between him and the guards, it began to seem the assignment had been a deliberate set-up for failure.

Other challenges materialized. One that created particular stress was his assignment to patrol the base, driving a patrol car on weekends, a 45 pistol at his side. Fortunately, he had a companion with him from time to time, and he started to learn how to answer the radio with the proper calls. The small-built Frenchman worried about the taller and bigger Americans who were inebriated, feisty, and ready for a brawl.

It had become obvious that he was not well-suited for the Military Police environment. His sergeant found a way to get him transferred out, this time to an overseas duty. There was no way to know if it would be Korea and its unstable situation. He would be required to take a military ship to an unknown destination.

Before he went overseas, Saint Pellicer had another chance to spend some time in Saint Louis. His parents were visiting his sister, Odette, and he was looking forward to reacquainting himself with friends and family.

Almost to Saint Louis, he experienced an unexpected delay. While rounding a bend, he lost control of his car, and landed in a field. A call to a friend who came to his assistance eased the predicament. It would turn out that the car needed more repairs than did he. A shaken yet grateful young man finally met up with his family.

Before long, it was time to leave Saint Louis again and report for his next duty. It would be on the long sea voyage out of New York before he would learn of his new destination.

This time his beloved car, by now repaired, stayed behind.

"Adventurous dangers often end in complete silence with a name engraved in solid marble."

On A Very Sharp Curve

At twenty-three,
I was returning
from Atlanta, Georgia,
for a new military assignment,
the undefined kind
with shipping orders.

Just outside of Saint Louis
it started raining.
I did not slow down
on a very sharp curve,
overly confident on dry pavement,
the slick wet highway, a new experience.
My immense Nash slid,
crossed the highway,
flew over the edge,
fell on four wheels into an embankment,
kept on bumping into the field,
forcing my foot on and off the gas pedal.

The driver's door was open.
By then, the car tried to eject me.
Frantic, I held on to the steering wheel,
my head hitting
repeatedly
the top of the door frame.

When it stopped,
my body was bruised,
with a concussion,
bumps on the head,
my arms stretched and in pain,
nerves shaken, completely disoriented.

I managed to drive the car back
onto the highway,
door not closing,
front body frame rubbing on the tires.
Cars and trucks passed by,honking
at my slow-moving pace.

A highway strip of gas station,
diner and the like
became the resting spot for the Nash.
I called a friend to be picked up,
taken to Saint Louis to my family.
This was nothing to tell by telephone.

My parents had arrived
from Europe.
In my excitement
my driving
was joyful,
reckless.

Always A Vagabond

His spirit always in unending chase
to faraway adventures in a new place.
It gave his heart a surge keeping him tense;
compelled, he would go over the last fence.

It took him no time to case the whole town,
a good eye cunning, never sporting a frown.
Friendly, he would find a gentle soul mate,
to stay there for a while, with a new date.

Never wrote notes to anyone he met.
He would call back, he made an assured bet.
Words from faraway were easy to say;
for him, writing was a hard price to pay.

Women who lost themselves in reveries
saw in his eyes demanding fantasies.
They knew with passion he would satisfy
the love found void that he would qualify.

To remain as free as a martingale,
ahead was more he wanted to inhale.
The mountains, the ocean, new encounters
unchallenged, only among freethinkers.

On his adventurous journey's last step
he is found back home, tall at the doorstep.
For a break, his heart waiting to be tense,
still in want to go over this old fence.

Always a vagabond
too free to correspond.
Always a vagabond.

Overseas
Panzer Kaserne

At Panzer Kaserne in Boeblingen, Germany, Saint Pellicer was assigned to the supply unit, a logical transition from his studies of quartermaster. Issuing military equipment to the soldiers and officers was the objective. It was a pleasant assignment. He shared a comfortable room with another soldier, in a building reminiscent of a castle. Due to their different time duties, they never saw each other. The objective was to keep both men apart from the troops at the dormitory to avoid friction that regulations put into the issuance of military gear. Demands for special treatment were often expected from soldier friends, a difficult situation.

The Military Entertainment Mecca

Dancing and acting were never far away from the young soldier's thoughts. Stuttgart was also not far away, and Saint Pellicer often went to town for the weekend dances at the USO. He took modern dancing lessons from German teachers and danced with a partner, a German girl, for ten months at weekend dances.

The Competition

A fellow soldier, intrigued with show business, was interested in entering a USO contest that could lead to an appearance on the Ed Sullivan Show, stateside. Having already recruited one soldier, he was looking to form a trio. In time, he noticed the talented dancer.

Uncertain what he was getting into, Saint Pellicer agreed to a meeting and a tryout. This led to forming the threesome – and many rehearsals. The comedy act could best be defined as an American Indian dance in file formation, a musical parody set to the words, *I've Got a Lovely Bunch of Coconuts* and *We Came a Long Way from Saint Louis.* Because of the historical nature of the theme and the improvisational and archaic treatment of the rhythms, the group aptly called themselves *The Primitives.*

The appreciative audiences of soldiers laughing and applauding at the nonsensical performance gave the group confidence that they had a good act. They won every competition until at last came the final competition that would determine the winning group who would appear on the Ed Sullivan show. The competition was held in Munich, and Olivia de Havilland was one of the judges.

In the end, first prize in comedy was awarded to the competitive group, *Damn Yankees.* Although, according to the actress, this was with some reluctance.

Years later, a 1960 story in the former *Saint Louis Globe-Democrat,* had this to say:

> "In Germany, as one of a trio called *The Primitives,* Saint Pellicer entered a European-wide dance competition for soldiers, at which Olivia de Havilland was a judge. Though the trio placed second, Mr. Saint Pellicer took comfort in the fact that the movie actress dissented – believing that the first prize should have gone to him and his colleagues."

Shows were usually well received by soldiers.

Elvis Presley, also in the Army during that time and stationed nearby, came to the base and performed in the immense lower level of the castle-like building where Saint Pellicer resided. More European-minded than American in musical tastes, he found Presley's style too wild, and did not understand the phenomenal impact that Presley had with music. So the young Frenchman did not bother to attend the concert, unaware that he was passing up the chance to see an entertainer well on his way to becoming enormously famous.

Back to the Real World, Military-Style

Following the competitions in the USO shows, the actor-soldier left Temporary Duty status and returned to the barracks. Because show business had taken him in a different direction, he was no longer seen as "one of them."

After a while, he transferred to another company on base. Unfortunately not much was happening, and he found the new assignment boring.

By now, he had only two months left in the service before his obligations were fulfilled.

It seemed an ideal time to use his accumulated vacation time to go to England for a few weeks where his parents were visiting his sister Josie and family. The visit provided a pleasant interruption from boredom in the waning days of his service.

Not long afterwards, the Army stint was over.

Military Epilogue

Initially, the Army had not been sure what to do with a young man who could not march in boots due to an earlier leg injury but who, conversely, could act and dance.

In the end, it seemed as though both the Army and Saint Pellicer were mutually satisfied with the outcome.

You Never Come Out As You Were

You never come out
from the Army
as you were.
You come out dismantled,
you reassemble your mind
and scrambled thoughts
the best you can,
on your own,
if you can.

You face the real world
from a different perspective.
Surprisingly
you do not belong
in it anymore.
It will not let you
back in it, just yet.

For you have changed.
You will have
to readjust
to normalcy.
When in – the Army
owns you entirely.
When out – the Army
abandons you.
After tampering with your life,
it offers no repairs
for the disruptions, the illogic
it has created.

Buddy, you are on your own
to fend for yourself
in the daily life
that has evolved since you left.
Early in Army days
you were considered a misfit.
Today in civilian life
you are again a misfit.

Saint Lou-ie, Saint Lou-ie

The Old Mississippi River muddy,
the blending Missouri River mighty,
the barges slowly fighting the current.
The lights on the bridge, glow, always present.
The shady trees hugging the streets gently,
the nearby country, forests, hills misty.

The cuisine you inhale lures to the Hill,
the Botanical Gardens orchids thrill.
Romantic autumn walks in the West End,
glancing at twin reflections in a blend
on the glass of French antique shop windows,
in love, finding their way to the bistros.

For here is where you find a chance to grow,
to create, to write, to shine your ego,
and then, ignoring you, of you let's go.
Pointing at bus stop, it ends there, Old Joe,
the shady trees hugging the streets gently,
the nearby country, forests, hills misty.

To find fame you must depart, go elsewhere
where no one is patient for an affair.
Where to mature there is no time, no yen,
where it must happen right, right there, right then.
Where everyone runs fighting the pressure,
where feelings must wear a suit of armor.

Saint Lou-ie, Saint Lou-ie will claim you back;
of you, will on radio for sometime yack,
full of pride, may even set up a star
along the sidewalks of artsy Delmar.

Saint Lou-ie, Saint Lou-ie, I will return.
Of sedate Midwest elegance I yearn.
Saint Lou-ie, Saint Lou-ie, I will return.
Saint Lou-ie, Saint Lou-ie, I will return.

Civilian Life and Saint Louis

"Freedom is abbreviated by laws, religions, customs, hang-ups."

With the military life behind him, the new civilian craved becoming part of the fifties, from a stateside point of view. Seated confidently at the steering wheel of his gleaming, chrome-embellished Nash Ambassador, the anticipative Saint Pellicer once again arrived in Saint Louis, this time for good.

In The Fifties

How proudly you washed your car in the street,
everyone with garden hose running, neat.
A bucket of water with suds, a sponge
in hand, bare arm ready for a deep plunge.

A long Nash with body like a bullet,
chrome bumper, white-wall tires near the gullet,
softly bleached by the sun, paint different hue,
maroon, metallic, original, new.

Tired after wash, the drying, the good scrub;
to make it shiny, hard wax is next rub.
Sweating, tee-shirt wet, hiding under tree,
for admiration of car, labor free.

A shower, a white shirt with tie, cufflinks,
smooth combed, stylish hair with lotion now blinks.
Drive-in Steak 'n Shake, tray on window to eat,
a Saturday's work must end with a treat.

In the fifties.

Career Choices

"Would you please repeat what you said?
I listen with a French accent."

Dance and Etiquette Instructor

Entertaining in the USO shows had whetted his lifelong appetite for the arts. Soon after his return, Saint Pellicer decided to pursue his original dream. It seemed a career in dance instruction would be something enjoyable, and would also provide physical activity. He applied at the Arthur Murray Dance Studio, where he was promptly hired. Following instructor training, he was teaching his own students within a week.

Not long afterwards, he received a telephone call from his sister Odette. Their mutual friend, Villa Duschene French teacher Madame Anne Marie de Moret, had recommended him to Mrs. Lemoine Skinner, who was interested in organizing dance and deportment classes for her younger children and their friends. Her preference was finding someone French, and someone with the style of the much beloved late Jacob Mahler, the last in a long line of Old World dancing masters. Mrs. Skinner seemed interested, and a meeting between Madame and Saint Pellicer was arranged.

Finding Madame Lemoine Skinner's home during the midst of a downpour proved daunting. Getting into Portland Place through the wrought iron gates, then on to the impressive mansion was another challenge. At last he found himself inside the foyer, and face to face with Madame. "I had thought you were not coming," she murmured, slightly perturbed. A hasty glance at the young man's drenched suit revealed a plausible explanation.

In spite of wet clothing and the delay, the meeting went well. Madame seemed pleased, and Saint Pellicer was hired. Before long, to the delight of Mrs. Skinner, the children were responding well, and she began recommending him to other friends. In no time, he was giving private classes in a rather large number of other homes as well.

Although all the children received dance lessons, only the youngsters got lessons in deportment. Older children were prone to believe they deported themselves well in social situations, so Saint Pellicer merely would weave it in without telling them.

The following story appeared in *The Saint Louis Globe-Democrat* regarding Saint Pellicer, entitled "Dancing Teacher – 1960 Style."

> "St. Louis society matrons are enthusiastically endorsing Mr. Saint Pellicer as a dancing and deportment teacher after a season in which he has taught principally in their homes. He is viewed as 'another Jacob Mahler' whose redoubtable efforts to teach dancing and the social niceties are still remembered. The late Jacob Mahler had taught, among others, thirty-six Veiled Prophet queens to face a dance floor rather than prefer to sink through it.
>
> "According to their mothers, St. Louis children, under the tutelage of Mr. Saint Pellicer, are inclining their heads – and their feet – in the direction he would have them go – and like it. It may be best explained by Saint Pellicer's comment that he is 'not going to repress that good forward attitude.' Yet, like the late Mr. Mahler, he insists on the formalities of decorous dress, receiving and departing lines, proper acceptances or refusals for dances, girls firmly escorted back to their chairs, duty dances, thank you to hostesses – in short, what he himself has acquired from a long line of proper French forebears."

Eventually he was instructing the children of Greenbriar Country Club members. Before long, adults were asking to be taught dance as well. *Greenbriar Country Club News* reported,

> "'Wonderful, lots of fun, getting better acquainted' were some of the remarks heard at the Friday Night Dance Get-togethers. Under the able guidance of Mr. Saint Pellicer, Teacher of Social and Deportment Styling, there is an exhibition of grace demonstrated within the group."

This led to dance instructions at Saint Louis Country Club, and classes for children at the Junior League tea rooms in the Frontenac. Adult dinner dances were held at Westborough Country Club, Old Warson Country Club, and Bellerive Country Club. Eventually his teaching venues would include the Kirkwood Cotillion at Algonquin Country Club and the Fleur de Lis dances at the Annunciata Church in Ladue.

In 1960, *Holiday* magazine carried an extensive feature on life in Saint Louis, where Saint Pellicer's classes were singled out with a photo.

That year also marked the beginning of new classes for Saint Pellicer. Fortnightlies were formed, and he was asked to instruct the Saturday Morning Classes, which would continue for a number of years. Patronesses for his classes included Mrs. Charles Bates, II, Mrs. Howard Benoist, Jr., Mrs. Bernard F. Desloge, Mrs. Donald J. Meyer, Mrs. Edward J. Mower, Jr., Mrs. Fristoe Mullins, Mrs. Joseph Pulitzer, Jr., Mrs. Thomas G. Rutledge, Mrs. Robert F. Schlafly, Mrs. Lemoine Skinner, Jr., Mrs. Edward D. Weekly, and Mrs. Louis Werner, II.

In December, Saint Pellicer was featured in *Ballroom Dance Magazine:*

> "Recognition of the importance of training young people to dance well and to behave attractively is a solid and long-established way of life in the upper stratum of St. Louis society. Sideline chaperones of present-day cotillions recall their own upbringing, and that of their parents. One teacher who is enjoying particular success in maintaining those traditions is a young man named Emil Saint Pellicer. One might expect that an inheritor of the Jacob Mahler mantle would have come from the city's Old Guard. Saint Pellicer, however, is of French descent, a native of Morocco, and has been a citizen of St. Louis for only six years. Dancing, which is but one of his many talents, came so naturally that he can't remember when he started."

In 1961, the *Globe-Democrat* reported that Saint Pellicer directed the Fleur de Lis Debutante Ball at the Khorassan Room at the Chase Park Plaza.

> "That year seventeen young women were presented to Cardinal-elect Joseph E. Ritter, Archbishop of St. Louis, in the last large party for the debutantes this season."

In October, The *Globe-Democrat* reported that Saint Pellicer directed both the elaborate French day production of *Promenade Along the Bridges in Paris* and the *Colorful Mexico* luncheon, at which he performed the Paso Doble. The two shows were represented in the *International Living Event*, a week-long affair featuring international lunches and performances, sponsored by Famous-Barr Company's Clayton store.

In 1962, Saint Pellicer was featured in a front-page article in the society section of the *Post-Dispatch* entitled *How St. Louis Children Learn Manners.* In it, heads from Villa Duchesne, Temple Israel, and Mary Institute, along with Saint Pellicer, were interviewed on the importance of good manners in today's society.

> "'To be absolutely comfortable, a well-bred person also needs the rituals of manners so firmly engrained that they are second nature to him,' said Saint Pellicer who conducts the Saturday Morning Dance Class at the Junior League Headquarters in Frontenac and who has inherited the mantle of the late Jacob Mahler. 'If children know exactly what to do, it builds their self-confidence.' Graduates at Mr. Saint Pellicer's classes have passed an awesome written examination."

After several seasons, it was suggested that perhaps the time had come for him to begin teaching at a place of his own. After all, Monsieur Mahler, he was told, had quite successfully taught his students in the ballroom of his fine mansion on Washington Boulevard in the Central West End, considered by many to be the ideal setting for instructing dance and deportment. Perhaps, Madame Skinner continued, he might find a similar place to continue the tradition.

Meanwhile, Linda Rand Orthwein on Westmoreland Place felt that her former home on Delmar would be just the perfect place for the young instructor. Knowing that the home was zoned for residential use, she hired an attorney who set about getting a variance. Alas, the board in University City would not hear of it, and so the plan for Delmar was abandoned.

Not long afterward, Saint Pellicer leased the ballroom in the Embassy building on Union Boulevard. It was an ideal place for instructing, and seemed to convey the spirit of the late Monsieur Mahler. Although it promised great potential, a cosmetic makeover was essential. So he quickly set to work decorating and adding many embellishments, including new chandeliers, mirrors and a fountain.

In no time, he had transferred his students to The Embassy where he continued to conduct classes, and began to host teas and receptions.

That Fall, the *France-Amerique* newspaper printed a story about his newly established Embassy Ballroom, which they termed a dancing salon.

In 1963 Saint Pellicer was interviewed and photographed by the *Globe-Democrat* as he was rehearsing at his Embassy Ballroom for an upcoming event entitled *Dancing – Now and Then.* The Missouri Historical Society was sponsoring the event in the Khorasssan Room of the Chase-Park Plaza. In a later article, the *Post-Dispatch* reported that Saint Pellicer had performed the Paso Doble.

The Embassy Ballroom became a meeting place for the Saint Louis chapter of the Alliance Française, an international French language and culture group. According to the *Globe-Democrat,* Fulbright Scholar Marc Goertz was the featured guest. Goertz was the official lecturer for the Alliance.

The Alliance Française ran a story about Saint Pellicer's dancing studio in the newly refurbished Embassy Ballroom.

During the Fall, the *Post-Dispatch* announced upcoming Saturday Morning Classes. A photograph showed Saint Pellicer interacting with his students in his ballroom.

Saint Pellicer hosted the French Troupe, Grand Ballet Classique, in his Embassy Ballroom, following a performance at Kiel Opera House, sponsored by the Alliance Française.

Andre Previn, composer, conductor and pianist, made his conducting debut in 1963 with the Saint Louis Symphony Orchestra. During his stay, Saint Pellicer became his designated host one afternoon, taking Previn on a tour of the City. When asked if he would like to visit the Embassy Ballroom, Previn indicated that indeed he would. And, they did.

In 1964, the *Post-Dispatch* reported that the Alliance Française had again met at the Embassy Ballroom. This time, world renowned French author Maurice Bruziere was the special guest.

And an article in the *Globe-Democrat:*

> "The Alliance Française will sponsor its second French Conversation Tea at the Maisonnette Française on the roof of the Chase-Park Plaza Hotel. Emil Saint Pellicer and Mrs. Newell Knight will be hosts."

Saint Pellicer, by now a member of the Board of Directors of the Alliance Française, was part of the group welcoming internationally renowned Maurice Chevalier to the French Maisonnette on a top terrace of the Park Plaza Hotel. It was a very special moment for the public, and for the members of the Alliance, to converse with the French singing star.

After several years at the Embassy, Saint Pellicer's initial efforts to decorate the ballroom proved to be his undoing. Alas, the landlord noticed all the embellishments that had been installed and, realizing its new potential, quickly tripled the rent. The dance master decided to search for another place.

Saint Pellicer's sister Odette again came to his assistance. She had noticed a two-story house for sale on Clayton Road that she thought might fit his needs. He had also noticed this house, but had felt there might be a zoning issue.

Nevertheless, he arranged to meet with the real estate agent to take a look. Beyond the pink walls and the pinker carpets, he could see the possibilities. Soon after, he cashed in some oil stock, and the house became his. This would double as his home and his fencing studio, or Salle d'Armes, which became known as the Saint Pellicer Conservatoire.

In September of 1964, both the *Post-Dispatch* and *Globe-Democrat* announced the grand opening of Saint Pellicer's Conservatoire.

The following year, Saint Pellicer announced a series of eight dinner dances to be held alternately at the Conservatoire, and at the Cheshire Inn.

Both the *Post-Dispatch* and *Globe-Democrat* reported that Saint Pellicer and Mrs. Pierce Powers had co-directed a series of summer French conversation classes sponsored by the Alliance Française to be held at the Maisonnette Française at the Chase-Park Plaza Hotel.

Again featured in *Ballroom Dance Magazine*, this time discussing his newly-created dance:

> "Saint Pellicer has come up with a new teenage dance, 'The Pelican,' which he created as a middle-of-the-road activity falling somewhere between the Twist and the Lindy-Hop swing dances. The twelve simple figures may be done in line or with couples. The dance will be performed by the Conservatoire Dancers on May 21 at the Grand International Ball which Saint Pellicer is coordinating for the Saint Louis Council on World Affairs."

A *Post-Dispatch* article reported the Annual Presentation of Awards for the Saturday Morning Class. The article included a photograph with the esteemed dancemaster and some of his patrons.

The *Globe-Democrat* reported that Saint Pellicer had coordinated the programs for the Grand International Ball held at the Khorassan Room at the Chase-Park Plaza Hotel.

From 1965 to 1966, he hosted a show on KFUO-FM Radio where he interviewed various folk singers and featured their performances.

In a story in the *Globe-Democrat*, Saint Pellicer was among several in Saint Louis to host ten European university students. The Council on World Affairs had arranged for this group to visit several universities here and other points of interest. Following a dinner in Gaslight Square hosted by the Alliance Française, Saint Pellicer hosted a party at his Conservatoire.

Harris Teachers College contacted Saint Pellicer to discuss the prospect of developing a course on etiquette to be included in their curriculum. They felt it would be beneficial for the students who were about to graduate and become teachers. He suggested that he would write a course on etiquette and present it to the teachers as a guide on what to teach their future students. This approach would avoid any resentment the prospective teachers may feel in being "told" what good manners were. His proposal was accepted by the college and became part of the curriculum that would reach thousands of students by way of their teachers.

Saint Pellicer seemed to have a knack for choosing fads that turned into careers at the most opportune times. His interest in fencing had begun years earlier while studying drama at the Conservatoire de Rabat as a young teenager, and his studies continued at Panzer Kaserne in Boeblingen, Germany while in the U.S. Army. Now it seemed the ideal time to add this classic sport to his deportment and dance instructions.

During the time that he resumed his fencing studies, Saint Pellicer was asked by society matron Anne Desloge Werner to produce a show with dancing, fencing, and fashions from Montaldos at Vouziers, the home castle of the Desloge family. The show went on in May, and included a number of dance numbers such as the Minuet, Gavotte, Polka, Waltz, Charleston, Tap Dance and Tango. Saint Pellicer and his dance partner performed the Cha Cha and the Paso Doble. As Madame had requested, the show also featured a fencing exhibition.

In the Fall of 1965 the *Globe-Democrat* reported his involvement in a Fencing Demo and a Hootenanny, presented at the Panorama '65 Fair, sponsored by radio station KFUO.

Later in the year, the new season of the Saturday Morning Dance Classes, now in its sixth year, was announced.

Vouziers On The Missouri Bluffs

As I entered the iron gates,
and drove up to the castle,
it became a different world,
a secluded enclave from France
overlooking the Missouri Bluffs.

It was a sunny day, clear skies,
the clouds chased away
in the comfortable warmth of mid-Spring,
a gentle breeze caressing
flowers and leaves.

The castle was on the left,
built of stones from the 17th century
brought back from France,
and gave an austere and grandiose
ambiance to elegant living.

An invitation from Grande Dame Anne Desloge
brought me there, wanting to show me the estate.
Traveling on horseback,
her arched back erect much like the heroines
from film epics, she led the way.

She insisted I had to mount a younger mare
who immediately realized I was no horseman,
afraid of heights, holding on his rein for dear life.
In command, its friskiness alive,
it was going to give me a ride to remember.

This must have been the customary tour
given new visitors to Vouziers.
Dame Anne, in the lead, galloped,
the other horses with guests followed;
miserably, for me, I placed at the end of the file.

I galloped along the narrow paths
dangerously close to the edge of the bluffs,
passing through an opening
cut into the stoned flank of the river,
too scared to look at the scenery.

I was preoccupied in staying secure on the saddle,
leaning over and hugging the neck
of the horse who felt it was in command
to pass the low clearings of the course,
rather than bypass taking another path.

The view was breathtaking,
the gallop was breathtaking,
the excitement was breathtaking,
making my heart pound at a high rate,
keeping me in a panic state.

We arrived at the underground ballroom
that was linked to the castle
through a long underground tunnel.
Guests of past walked along a gallery of paintings
on the way to the dance floor.

Its stone entrance reminiscent
of a stately structure in a Parisian garden,
built into the hill with oversized French doors
spanning its facade, letting daylight come in
'til dark, when candles romanticized the soiree.

There, about to take place,
an afternoon at Vouziers,
a gala of dance, fencing bouts,
modeling of clothes from Montaldos
with a cast of socialites and performers.

Fencing Career Hatched

Saint Pellicer enjoyed a successful fencing career, spanning over fifteen years. Press coverage was frequent and too numerous to detail here. Although some articles have been lost, over forty remain and are listed on Pages 236-237. Following are excerpts from a few:

In 1963, the *St. Louis County Observer* reported that Saint Pellicer continued his studies by attending seminars at Notre Dame University and at other events. As he pursued his studies in fencing, the busy entrepreneur continued his dance and deportment classes in Saint Louis.

In 1965-66, Saint Pellicer studied with Yucel Erden, the Turkish Sabre Champion, and member of the Turkish Olympic Fencing Team. He took Master classes from Georgio Santelli, former United States Olympics Fencing Coach. This required numerous trips to New York City. The revered master conducted these sessions entirely in French. After a series of skills testing, Saint Pellicer perfected a teaching technique that earned him the title of Maitre D'Armes.

In 1968, *Sunday Pictures* magazine of the *Post-Dispatch* printed a feature article about Saint Pellicer entitled, "Dueling For Sport." In the article, Saint Pellicer explains that the object of a fencing duel is to touch your opponent without being touched in return. Quips the article's author, "In this way, he assures his students, very few heads get cut off."

The article includes a number of photos taken at his fencing school showing some of the standard poses, such as the art of thrusting and parrying, the "riposte," the "salut" and the "fender."

One photo shows four students from Connecticut, Kansas, New Jersey, and Rhode Island saluting Saint Pellicer at the beginning of the class. In another, Saint Pellicer corrects a Webster Groves High School student as she holds the foil in the extension position. In another, that student lands a straight foil thrust to a student from New York. Another student is shown attempting a cut to the head, but the Master parries the cut with his sabre, bringing the fencers to *corps à corps*. Both men are dressed in full fencing regalia.

Also included are photos of a two-handed sword and a rapier, part of Saint Pellicer's collection of old weaponry.

The article concludes with Saint Pellicer, who is a fencing coach at Saint Louis University, saying that students come to him to learn mental alertness, as well as physical adroitness.

An article and photo in the 1973 Jan 27 – Feb 2 *TV Guide*:

"TV Facts Salutes Emil Saint Pellicer. The Saint Pellicer Conservatoire is located in the metropolitan St. Louis area. Men and women duelists, young and not so young from the city and the county, even from Chicago and Indiana, often from Europe and South America, meet and sharpen their skill. Athletic dueling in the round started right here at the Conservatoire. Dueling Master Emil Saint Pellicer invented the electronic daggers and shields as well as a system that is unique in the world. The master's personality is everywhere; he has planned every detail from décor to instruction, daggers to electronics."

In Bob Goddard's column in the *Globe-Democrat*, Jan. 30, 1973:

"Here and There: Latter-day D'Artagnan – Local "Dueling Master" Emil Stanley Saint Pellicer, who made his 34th television appearance on the Regis Philbin Show Saturday, is also much in demand 'round town for demonstrations and lectures on 'Athletic Dueling' and 'History of Swords and Armor.' For extra info, better check with the local chapter of the American Athletic Dueling Association."

From the March 2, 1973 *Rutgers Observer*:

"Michael Faulkner accepts Rutgers University Outstanding Athlete Award. Faulkner has one hundred victories and only nine defeats as a member of the Rutgers Fencing Team. Faulkner, a student of Emil Saint Pellicer before joining the Rutgers Fencing Team, returns to St. Louis and joins again the Saint Pellicer Conservatoire to prepare himself and compete in Athletic Dueling."

The following article appeared in September, 1974, *Apartment Living.*

"Emil Saint Pellicer thinks himself as an educator first; a Maitre d' Armes, dueling master, second. Moroccan-born Saint Pellicer has from 65 to 85 students in his school intent on becoming accomplished fencers or Athletic Duelers. The soft-spoken Frenchman should know something of the latter since he invented the modern version of the sport. Athletic Dueling differs from fencing in that matches are fought in the round as opposed to being fought in a formal squared-of area. Saint Pellicer, while still teaching fencing, 'because people want it,' has turned his main interests to athletic dueling. 'I did a lot of research on it and found that the ancient Aztecs and Mayans fought in the round,' he says. Saint Pellicer's sport has already met with some success. St. Louis University and UMSL have programs and several universities in New York, Tennessee and Ohio are interested in it. Not only has Saint Pellicer invented a sport but he has developed some accoutrements of that sport, namely the electronic dagger, shield, and an electronic trainer.

"One of Saint Pellicer's favorite words is 'freedom.' He speaks of it in regard to life as well as fencing. 'Fencing,' he says, 'is so formal, so ritualistic and that's why I've gotten so deeply into athletic dueling.' In a moment of self-revelation, Saint Pellicer made this observation about himself: 'At one time I was a perfectionist – everything had to be just so – and, believe me, I was not free. By being so formal, the enjoyment went out of the sport,' he adds."

The following article along with photos appeared in the April 2, 1975 *St. Louis Globe Democrat:*

"Several high schools and colleges in the St. Louis area teach the fundamentals of fencing for the virtue of the art in promoting posture and coordination as well as the exercise involved. Even a large St. Louis corporation encourages its employees to participate in the sport. One of the principal advocates in St. Louis for perpetuating and teaching the art of fencing and dueling is Emil

Saint Pellicer who operates the Saint Pellicer Conservatoire or fencing academy on Clayton Road. Saint Pellicer is an athletically trim person with black hair and a short beard peppered with gray. His posture is straight and his movements are graceful. His appearance is that of a man who is either a fencing master or a dancing teacher – both in which he has engaged.

"Instructions are given at the Academy in the use of the small sword, epee, sabre, rapier and dueling baton. Several students attend the academy on the recommendation of their physicians for the purpose of improving their coordination, Saint Pellicer said. The difference between fencing and dueling, according to Saint Pellicer, is that the former is more stylized where the opponents approach each other from a frontal position. Dueling allows for more mobility in which the attack can be from either side as well as frontal."

The list of schools where Saint Pellicer instructed is quite extensive: He was a Fencing Coach at John Burroughs High School; Maitre d'Armes at Saint Louis University and Forest Park Community College; and he taught classes ranging from "The Influence of the French in Fencing," "The Duels," "Electronic Fencing," "History of Fencing From Antiquity to Today," to "Seminar on the Foil" and "Techniques of the Bouts," at Lindbergh and Clayton High Schools; Washington University, De Andreas and Ferguson High Schools; Florissant Valley Junior College; Notre Dame and Lutheran South High Schools, all in Saint Louis; Westminster College in Fulton, Missouri; Belleville High 12 Club in Belleville, and Southern Illinois University in Edwardsville, both in Illinois.

During his years at the Conservatoire, Saint Pellicer established a long friendship with Dr. Michael Fox. Dr. Fox came to the Conservatoire for fencing practice on club nights. A veterinarian, Fox would go on to become a nationally acclaimed syndicated columnist. He recently confided, "As an Englishman, I feel that Saint Pellicer brought a spark of Old Europe to enrich, if not civilize, the Midwest."

Driving by the Conservatoire on Clayton Road, one could often see the fencers, in white attire and helmets, in bouts on the front platform of the house. There would be numerous calls of "En Garde!" from passing drivers who would lower their windows to shout it out.

By this time, Saint Pellicer's parents had moved permanently to the United States, and the family was once again reunited in Saint Louis. These were good years for Saint Pellicer. His fencing credentials had brought him national status.

In addition to being featured regularly in newspaper and magazine articles, Saint Pellicer also made nearly three dozen appearances on the Regis Philbin Show, which at that time was produced in Saint Louis. He was also a frequent guest on Jack Carney's radio program. His numerous television appearances also included KSD-NBC, KMOX-CBS, KTVI-11 and KDNL-30. He conducted a number of radio interviews on stations KFUO, KMOX, KSD, WRTH, KXOK, KRCH, and KSHE.

He was a frequent guest on the Charlotte Peters Show, discussing a range of topics. He would typically receive a call from the producers asking him to prepare for an interview on a particular topic. More often than not, the topic for which he had prepared would never come up, and he and Peters would instead embark on a completely different subject. He learned early on that Peters liked to be challenged. It was better to be assertive and to even interrupt during these on-set interviews.

Over the years Saint Pellicer had become a beloved figure in Saint Louis society and with the media. In a piece entitled *Life at the Chase-Park Plaza During the Bicentennial of Saint Louis*, Saint Pellicer is photographed along with Mrs. Harold Koplar, Mrs. Bernard Ehrenreich, Mrs. James Dodds, Mrs. Louis Werner II, and others at a reception given by the French Commercial Counselor, the French Consul and the Alliance Française.

An Inventor

Meanwhile, Saint Pellicer's interest in research relating to the sport of fencing had led to a collection of patents. So impressed was acquaintance John Culling, Chairman of Carondelet Foundry, with what he described as a genius for inventions, that he provided the imaginative Saint Pellicer his own laboratory within the foundry.

In a *University News* article March 14, 1975:

"Here at Saint Louis University, Athletic Dueling is made even more interesting, as students are instructed by one of the most skilled duelists in the country, Dueling Master Emil Saint Pellicer. Saint Pellicer calls dueling an American sport. 'Americans demand realism with a fair and logical code to follow,' he states. 'They like the charisma of romanticism in weaponry, but they demand electronic computing of the results that are too fast for the human eye to judge fairly.' The issue of fair judging has been eliminated by Saint Pellicer, as he has built a new computer to register the scoring results.

"At present, he holds six patents on equipment he has designed. All the weapons are electronic. When touched with the weapon, the computer registers the point. Points are accumulated against you, which makes the sport a little more offensive than defensive, but the skill of both is required if one expects to become like the Dueling Master Saint Pellicer."

In an April 2, 1975 *Saint Louis Globe Democrat* story and photographs:

"Saint Pellicer also gives fencing instructions to employees of the Carondelet Foundry once a week. The foundry has provided a fencing area in one of its buildings where employees practice swordsmanship during their lunch hour or after work. John H. Culling, chairman and president, has 20 employees who are interested in the sport. 'Most companies have some sort of team activity for their employees,' Culling said, 'and we feel this is one where they can have fellowship and competition as well as a good physical conditioner.' He pointed out that about one-half hour of fencing is equivalent to playing two sets of singles tennis. Culling said some of the older executives of the plant were preparing to enter the Senior Olympics to be held next year."

In an article and photograph that appeared in the *Saint Louis Post-Dispatch* on July 25, 1975:

"The art of Athletic Dueling, as shown above by Dueling Master Stanley Saint Pellicer, right, and John H. Culling, Board chairman of Carondelet Foundry, will be just one of the featured exhibitions during the 'Moonlight Jamboree' on Maryland Plaza until midnight or later, according to Alfonso J. Cervantes, president of the Maryland Plaza Redevelopment Corporation, sponsor of the affair. Saint Pellicer is Dueling Master at St. Louis University and Culling is president of the American Athletic Dueling Assn. Along with demonstrations of various dueling weapons, a demonstration will be given on the use of the baton, umbrella and cane as defense weapons. The event will be emceed by the legendary Harry Fender, radio and TV personality."

Summer

*"Once we have matured beyond the
idealistic assumptions of youth
we mellow into a more practical perspective."*

There Is Sun Overhead

*There is sun overhead.
The surprising Summer night left a cool ground
for a welcome lull.*

*No way to predict when the blistering rays
will return to scorch nature and our spirits.
It could be as early as noon.*

*I enjoy the early morning hours
just after the longest day
brings early light when I open one eye.*

*In disbelief, I open the other one
and ask myself, "What am I doing here,
in bed, when the splendid day is already on its way?"*

*There is so much to do or not to do
for I would like to celebrate
a day that is so promising with plain languor.*

There is sun overhead.

Courtship and Marriage

"Love is an illusion, at its best in a dream."

At the peak of his patent acquisitions, fencing career and country club involvements, a woman entered his aura of consciousness, and into his life. He was impressed with her beauty, and with her flair for stylish clothes.

We Danced All Night

Just there, on the patio, the music started.
You were there, petite,
an elegance I had only dreamed,
a smile, the smile of a person happy with herself.
Simply, you said your name;
simply, I said my name.

It was meant that we would lift our arms
to hold and dance right there
to swingy music rhythms breaking away,
giving a chance to see you whole,
a delight.

We danced all night;
We danced all night.

Their lavish wedding took place in 1967 at Le Chateau. But not before the lifelong Catholic Saint Pellicer was compelled by her family to complete another round of Catholic instructions. To be a French Catholic had not been Catholic enough!

Loss of Mother

Maria Gracia Sanchez Padilla

"Life is of changes."

Sadly, Saint Pellicer's mother died shortly before the wedding. She would never meet her beloved son's future in-laws.

Tears When Thinking Of You

I shed tears when thinking of you
from far away beyond the sea,
in time, my heart wrapped in iron,
hiding my love for you, full of faith.

I shed tears when thinking of you,
in my young years, leading me by the hand
on return from school when I was hungry,
all my trifles from day had lost their weight.

I shed tears when thinking of you,
now departed, is not the end.
I keep a handkerchief to dry my sorrow,
awaiting the echo of words from the past.

I will shed tears every somber day,
we will be together as free as we wish,
not having to please anyone, ever,
past and reflections protected in the shade.

Opened is my love for you, full of faith,
awaiting the echo of words from the past.
Maman and me.
Maman and me.

Above the Conservatoire

*"Love in a dream we can shape.
Awake, we cannot manage it."*

After the wedding and a honeymoon to Canada, they settled in together above the Conservatoire.

She was not interested in his country club set, and in time, his involvement with the organizations he belonged to dwindled.

In many ways the couple could not have been more incompatible, and their decision to marry would have a profound impact that would resonate for many years to come.

Meanwhile, Saint Pellicer's artistic career in Saint Louis, now in its tenth year, continued to prosper.

Oh, Listen

*Oh, listen to me again and again
as I formulate my thoughts aloud
over problems and decisions
that are hard to trace.*

*Accept my projects,
my hopes and failures,
knowing that just your presence
will hold me on until the next
fortune, or crash.*

Birth of First Daughter

Suzanne Almarie Saint Pellicer

"I want to be myself; think for myself;
do for myself; be by myself.
Myself."

On March Twentieth

On March Twentieth I think of Spring
the blue skies and the sunshine to bring.
The birds prepare their cozy nest
with twigs, feathers and what they find best.

It is the time for songs and happy days,
for bees to work while they pursue their plays
from petal to petal, a flower at a time,
their wings buzzing in perfect rhyme.

On March Twentieth I think of Spring
the blue skies and the sunshine to bring,
the fond memories when you were born
when you stopped my heart from being forlorn.

Along the years you have kept your radiant smile,
its warmth makes me go the extra mile
that a father will take for his daughter,
to write how grand she is, for he is a writer.

Birth of Second Daughter

Aimee Celine Saint Pellicer

"Do not fashion me to your standards;
I will not fit. I will rebel."

Let The Last One Go By With A Cheer

Memory replays a bright early year
of a child happy, alert and cheerful.
A gracious daughter growing, always dear;
a charming young woman, rarely tearful,
the delight of a proud father.

Just about to start is another year;
soon time will demand to slow down rather
than let the last one go by with a cheer.
Celebrate this day, a wonderful life
with your father's many a wish sincere.

Always A Leader

My child was always a leader.
She would at recess round up a
few students and march them
to the nearby train station on
their way to a new city.

Abb
Vaughn

Dueling Master's Successes

In a 1973 story in the *Saint Louis Globe-Democrat*:

> "Men and women duelists everywhere, often from Europe and South America, meet and sharpen their skills. Athletic dueling in the round started right here in the Conservatoire. Dueling Master Emil Stanley Saint Pellicer invented the electronic daggers and shields as well as a system that is unique in the world. The Master's personality is everywhere, he has planned every detail from décor to instruction, daggers to electronics…"

The following entitled *En Garde! Emil Saint Pellicer* appeared in *Apartment Living* in September, 1974:

> "There's a private side to Emil Saint Pellicer and it mainly concerns itself with his lovely wife and their two daughters, Aimee Celine, age two, and four-year-old Suzanne. 'I am sorry that more people aren't bi-lingual, and so with that in mind, I only speak French to the girls,' he says. Saint Pellicer's father has assisted in decorating their living quarters above the school in a most charming, quaint manner. There is no question that it would indeed be worthy as a feature in *Apartment Living*. They've built walls, put up interesting touches here and there.
>
> "It was suggested that if he were not already a top-flight dueling master, he would make a first-rate interior designer. At this, Saint Pellicer shrugged, and the interview came to a close."

According to a 1975 article in the *Globe-Democrat* and with a nod to something that would become a much later trend:

> "Saint Pellicer explained, 'In the arts, there is an interest in having one's own building and having more flavor of oneself in it.' Saint Pellicer, his wife and two children live above the studio. 'Were I not here at home, I would not be able to see my children. I have a closer relationship with my family and see them more often this way, even though one place is completely private from the other.'"

A Chink in the Armor . . . Goodbye to Clayton

*"When your task is to please someone,
you have lost mastery of your life.
You have become a slave."*

After almost ten years of living over the Salle d'Armes, his wife longed for a life in the suburbs. Saint Pellicer worried that the distance from the City presented a potential conflict for the successful fencing career. Yet, in the end, Saint Pellicer parlayed what had been his home and studio for nearly fifteen years into a new house in the far away suburbs. The Conservatoire relocated to a plaza, not far from where the new home would be.

No one could have imagined what a negative impact the move would have on Saint Pellicer's life – or on his storybook career, now in its twentieth year.

It did not take very long to realize that his fears had materialized. The new location was too far away to lure steady clients from the more artistically centered City. Frustrated, he expressed his disappointment in a poem, aptly entitled, *Stanley est mort.* His long fencing career had come to an end – along with the use of the name Stanley.

Stanley est mort

Stanley est mort, tué par sa femme,
éteint est son esprit et sa flamme,
descendu, blessé, de sa tour de gloire,
de succès il ne pourra plus en boire.

Stanley est bien mort, il n'est plus
à oublier est ce qu'il fut.

Stanley est mort tué par sa femme,
par une âme jalouse qui blâme
tourmentée, rongée par triste rancoeur
un profond silence tranchant, railleur.

Stanley est bien mort, il n'est plus
à oublier est ce qu'il fut.

There Is A Drought

For ideas, it has been necessary to scramble;
my hopes for enough poems for a booklet ramble.
The drought is not only a weather concern;
schemes are dry in the day and stubbornly nocturne.

It is an exercise for doing something
with the obvious of having nothing.
The torrid air inflames the soul and stops all.
Being boxed in makes me wish for fall.

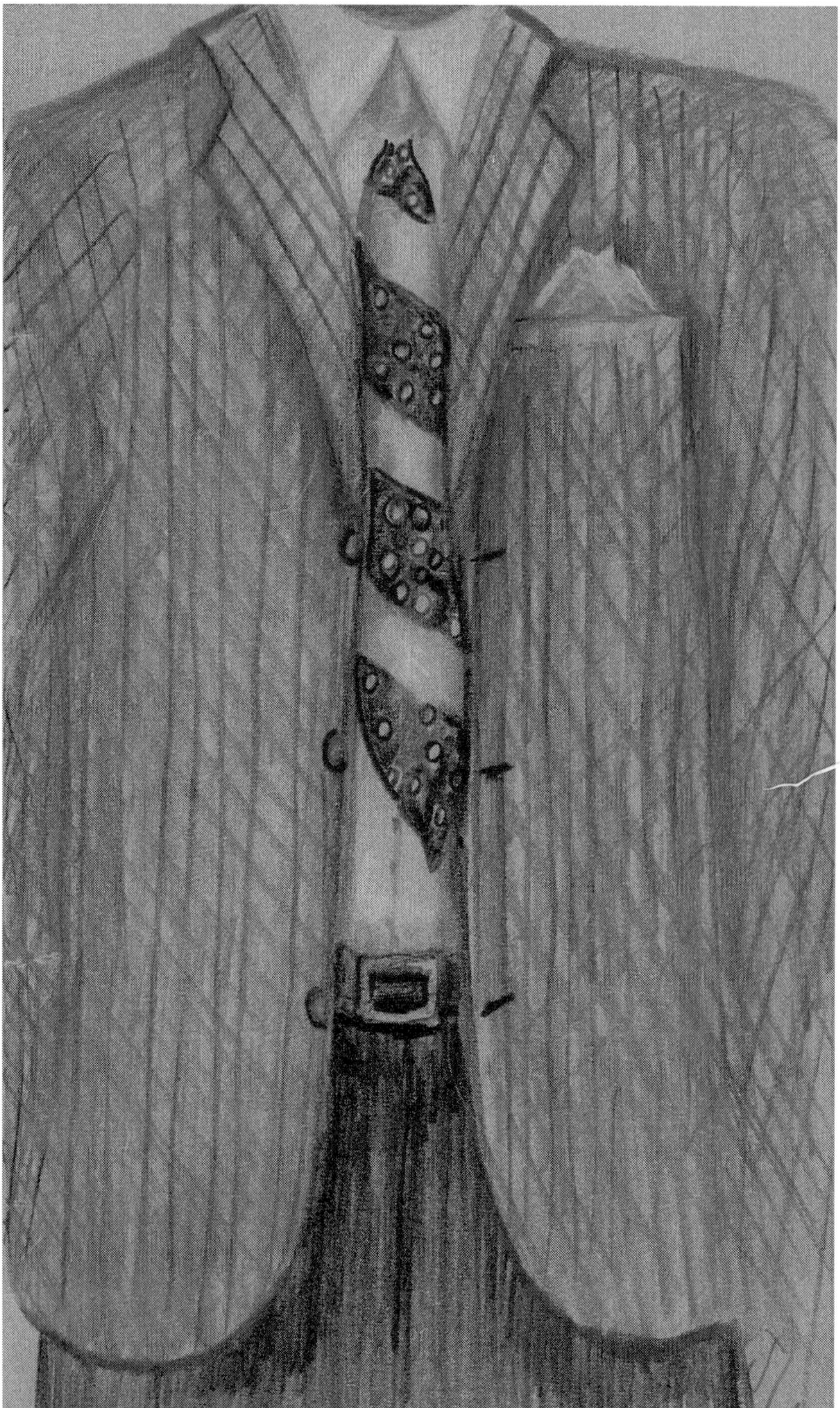

From Artistic… to Administrative

*"My thoughts in my mind are well organized;
my memory in the computer is well classified.
Only my desk will make you think otherwise."*

Accustomed to a long career in the art world, the more available administrative jobs in the suburbs fell flat. But the resourceful Saint Pellicer drew from his past – he was proficient in Spanish, French and English – and he returned to teaching, tutoring and translating.

By then, the computer age was in full swing. For Saint Pellicer, computers were just another language, and it seemed only natural to begin taking courses.

It Was Monday

*What a day it was; it was long and dragging
as if it were endless.
Every minute lasted twice as long,
a length without an end.*

*Internal aggravation
could not be shown.
It is so much unlike me.
Or is it?*

*Camouflages
are what we learn when young.
We show patience to others
while, inside, we are irritated, exhausted.*

*What a day it was.
It was Monday.*

Loss of Father

Raymond Saint Pellicer Bonancia

Saint Pellicer's father died during this time. In later years he at times stayed with the family, and was much appreciated and beloved.

An Angelic Haze

I dreamed of a bright haze descending
into the room at his bedside,
an angelic touch to his arm,
a call to the perennial gardens,
a call to a forever Spring.

Papa was there in bed.
He wanted to talk
as he could,
a faint voice still strong
with the inflection that gave him away
on the telephone.

I heard, "It is time for me to leave;
the battle has ended.
It is overdue for me to rest, for you,
and the victor as well."

Agony gripped my chest.
I wanted to say, "Don't go yet!"
But then I didn't.
Father always knew best.
Yes, exhausted he needed a rest.

He closed his eyes, stopping his breath.
He stretched his body and let go,
a smile on his face for he saw me there
holding his hand over my breast.

I leaned over and kissed him on the forehead.
"Goodbye, Papa, thank you for my life,
for the joy of laughter we shared,
a child happy, dancing in your arms."

He said, "It is time for me to leave;
the battle has ended.
It is overdue for me to rest, for you,
and the victor as well."

I dreamed of a bright haze descending
into the room at his bedside,
an angelic touch to his arm,
a call to the perennial gardens,
a call to a forever Spring.

I dreamed an angelic haze lifting his hand,
an angelic haze claiming his soul,
an angelic haze now in the sky;
an angelic haze high in the sky.

A House Divided

*"A love without trust and respect leads to divorce.
A marriage without trust and respect will survive no love."*

It has been said that opposites attract. Perhaps this was true in the beginning for the Saint Pellicers. But, over time, the pragmatism and ingrained austerity of her former convent life seemed to clash with his artistic nature and Old World culture.

They were two people with very different backgrounds, interests, concepts, and goals. And they were growing further apart.

Ignore The Ghost

Autumn with cool weather now turning fate,
gone yesterday's warm Indian Summer day
with sparse clouds, dreary sky now of grey,
an even light over the hills quite late.

Nothing there to lift our spirit with joy;
instead, awakened, is a time to think
about the past much longer than a blink,
pondering what led to this dismal ploy.

We were all divorced, each story a bore,
still the disaster years hold on for most.
Good days can return; ignore the ghost
so that sad moments, past, will come no more.

We must warm up from the descending chills;
with relationship gone, the mind is free
to linger into a discovering spree.
In silence, let's walk up the rolling hills.

Midlife Crisis

*"A brick of lead is safe
unless it is chained to your neck
and you are under water."*

It was during this difficult period that Saint Pellicer, who was then a college director, found himself a victim of downsizing, and without a job. Most small colleges were caught in this trend; what had once been a lucrative career now offered very little in employment opportunities.

During his unemployment, their marriage disintegrated further, and divorce proceedings began. This would lead to the dissolution of a relationship that had endured for over twenty-three years.

Formulated

You formulated a question.
You formulated an expectation.
You formulated a response.
You formulated my answer.
You formulated yourself out of my life!

This is a straight unformulated goodbye,
before you formulate my mind.

The Bitter Winds Of Chesterfield

Wrangling, the bitter winds of Chesterfield
come across the expanse of gone wheat field.
They grip, they snake to reach the new highways
where lands have been cleared for faddish pathways.

Cunning, the bitter winds of Chesterfield
whisper between manses to never yield,
whistling, hugging the front of each doorstep
over rooms lined up in a man-made steppe.

Flirting, the bitter winds of Chesterfield
forge the countryside as a vast playfield.
Before you know it, they start with a tease;
soon you feel the cold and its coming freeze.

Pompous, the bitter winds of Chesterfield!
Everything is grandiose for the well heeled,
for nothing is ever more than a breeze
when the high heating bills you can appease.

Winning, the bitter winds of Chesterfield
are forceful, cunning in their battlefield.
They whisper, they whistle, they tease, they swirl;
to the trees' fallen leaves they give a whirl.

The Fallout

*"There is a bastard born every minute
and it is not out of wedlock."*

The early nineties continued to be bitter for Saint Pellicer who, for all of his life, had never been deprived of anything. Now, with the divorce final and out of his home, finding another place to live was his highest priority. Jobs were difficult to come by, and this had quickly translated into meager surroundings.

The situation became increasingly critical as the divorce settlement languished.

Growing desperation and chronic unhappiness continued. The day would come when he would surely regard this period in his life as the lowest.

To Rent Is An Awful Step

*You never know if the previous renting ace
had one pet, or enough to fill up a zoo.
Four-legged animals that mark their space,
eradicating fumes requires a cleaning crew.*

*Three weeks of the worst allergies went by;
no medicine would help my nose's wrath.
Nasal medicine refused to turn dry;
no relief for my constant drip bath.*

*A gamble to rent is an awful step.
Expect a long time for locals to vent.
Before moving in, do finish the prep;
a clean-up job first is money well spent.*

And
God
Bless
Us
Every one!

"Some will see to it
that you feel worse than they do.
This will make them feel better."

The Rental Agent's Motto

Don't send tenant's check through a second time;
it may clear, and you will not make a dime.
Show rental papers; firm you stand, you say,
no logic, anything to have your way.
Whatever the note may be in the contract,
ignore, if he shows his rights you infract.

For good measure, raid his thin wallet clean
for your coffers; let's pluck the tenant lean.
First, levy twenty dollars for the check bounce.
Then, add a twenty-five for an extra pounce.
Send a note citing, "It is a felony
to give a bounced check here in Missouri."

Then be happy you turned his life affray,
for your chicanery gives you good pay.

Saint Pellicer continued to wait for his divorce settlement. By now, several years had passed since the divorce. The decree had allowed her to remain in the house, and it was a matter of waiting until she moved, before a sale could take place.

Because of his precarious situation – no decent job and little income – he was forced to accept at times offers that he hoped had come with sincerity from the kindness of strangers.

Instead, all too often he found himself a victim of opportunists.

During Hard Times

Thank you for making my life much better
when my despair was at a high meter;
no glue, no tape could help make it easy,
an uncertain hold, so fragile, so queasy.

Kindness, understanding, then there is more;
a look saying "we appreciate" helps galore!
A smile when the going is getting tough
does heal a soul tired of unending gruff.

Life gets tangled in long strands, malicious,
tortuous, ambivalent, oblivious;
it remolds our feelings with such harshness
often to the point of break without noblesse.

On your request, your kind gift will be spent
on a computer update, to the last cent.
It has suffered just as a human with scars,
silent, impassive, when not up to par.

Departing Rat

Upon your departure let's wish you well.
A hole in the ground, thirty feet down,
water to chin, a strong echo, a bell;
the key things you need to repent, or drown.

Only after cleansing your nasty mind
should you be allowed up to the light.
On your knees, swearing you have become kind,
knowing, if not, there goes a down flight.

Now your nightmares will drive you crazy
with the black angel next to, touching you,
wrapping the abrasive you in cloud hazy,
with delight he will give you the change due.

Hell will wait, its bellows of fire and smoke,
no need to rush to your new flaming town.
Stay here on earth to bear and choke
on flashbacks turning you upside, then down.

Rat!

Looking For Happiness

Looking for happiness, unending quest,
never without flaws, always quick to tear.
Search for woods, cabin, silence, bliss and rest,
for human specimen, flowing blond hair.

Consumed, uncomfortable, empty nest.
Love ended, hideaway no more the thing.
The human became an unwanted pest,
the blond hair fallen straight down as white string.

Silence lost to birds, crickets, frogs out west,
it is always greener over the fence,
hang-ups isolating our minds at best,
confusing ourselves, thoughts making no sense.

Like a flood, our riddles come to a crest
with a damaging regress to their banks.
Life continues, bland, having lost some zest,
fighting on, new hang-ups each day still cranks.

The Remains of the Day

"Promises are always beyond what one can hold on to."

The divorce settlement still in limbo, father and daughters continued piecing together the broken shards of the past.

To My Daughters

Our lives are of chapters, each with a different title, each one within a different cycle that has the tendency to reappear. In those cycles that seem unbearable, know that the next cycle is bound to be greater, happier. Bathe your mind with the positive; enjoy the sunset; look at the glistening waters that ripple on a summer evening as the sun dips into the horizon to end a day. Enjoy the start of everything, accept the happenings of the day, and relax with the evening setting. Let the difficulties pass on; do not attach yourself to them. Resolve them and move on.

You are the most precious happening into the life of a father who adores you. Let this fatherly love bring warmth to your spirit. Know that your grandfather held you in his arms when he almost never held his own children. Know that your grandmother would have held you in her arms with the same love she had for your father, and the pride that you were her grandchildren. You have love all around you; let it come into your spirit.

From the deepest of my heart.

Avec tout mon amour
Papa

Today You Are Twenty-One

Awaiting today to be twenty-one
into the world, ready, you want to soar
with apprehension and joy, all-or-none,
a new challenging life, a boat to oar,
the happy journey is starting today.
I am asking all of the stars to light
so that you will never feel left at bay
on your way with hope, a guided path bright.

Always Sunshine After The Rain

You will be proud of yourself as
you seem to get closer to your objective.
Hold on, you are almost there.
I can understand the strain just now.
What counts is seldom easy.
Keep on trucking 'til a break in the dark clouds.
There is always sunshine after the rain.

Weaned!

My mother weaned me early from her arm
where I was comfortable for so long.
Father never held us, wanting no harm.
We were small, and he was ever so strong.

To my children I was an older chap,
a father, never wavering with care.
Joyful, I held them often on my lap,
playful, crawled around with them, everywhere.

Until you were eighteen you were so close
with the presence of pure fatherly love.
Happily in pictures we would both pose;
between us could not come dissent nor shove.

Then came college, changes, as time went by;
so hard adjusting to less attention.
You were much the grownup, not knee-high,
away, wanting a new life extension.

With time can grow nonchalance, you know.
Silence, distance have taken us apart;
communications have reached a new low
to be estranged by a major rampart.

The main culprit is mostly the divorce;
in their confusion children take sides.
Wounded, high I still ride my warhorse,
hurt and unable to go with the tides.

Weaned!

Moment Alone

To have a moment alone,
away from mother and other kin,
a lone detail flared, anger sewn,
lamenting what should have been.

We have long matured to debate
the things we know can never change.
We conclude it is often fate
that leads us astray, makes us strange.

We almost give ultimatums,
"you do this, or I do that,"
ignoring moratoriums,
and postponing, go to bat.

We sit back to relax,
so pleased that we are just two;
we need to put away our axe
and our cutting words, too.

Admiration is what links us,
kindness, compassion, close ties.
These are what allow us to fuss,
our love never permitting lies.

We feel better after a storm;
on that we can count, we both know.
Our attitudes are back to norm;
a hug with smiles lets our love flow.

Smiles let our love flow.
Flow, grow, know.

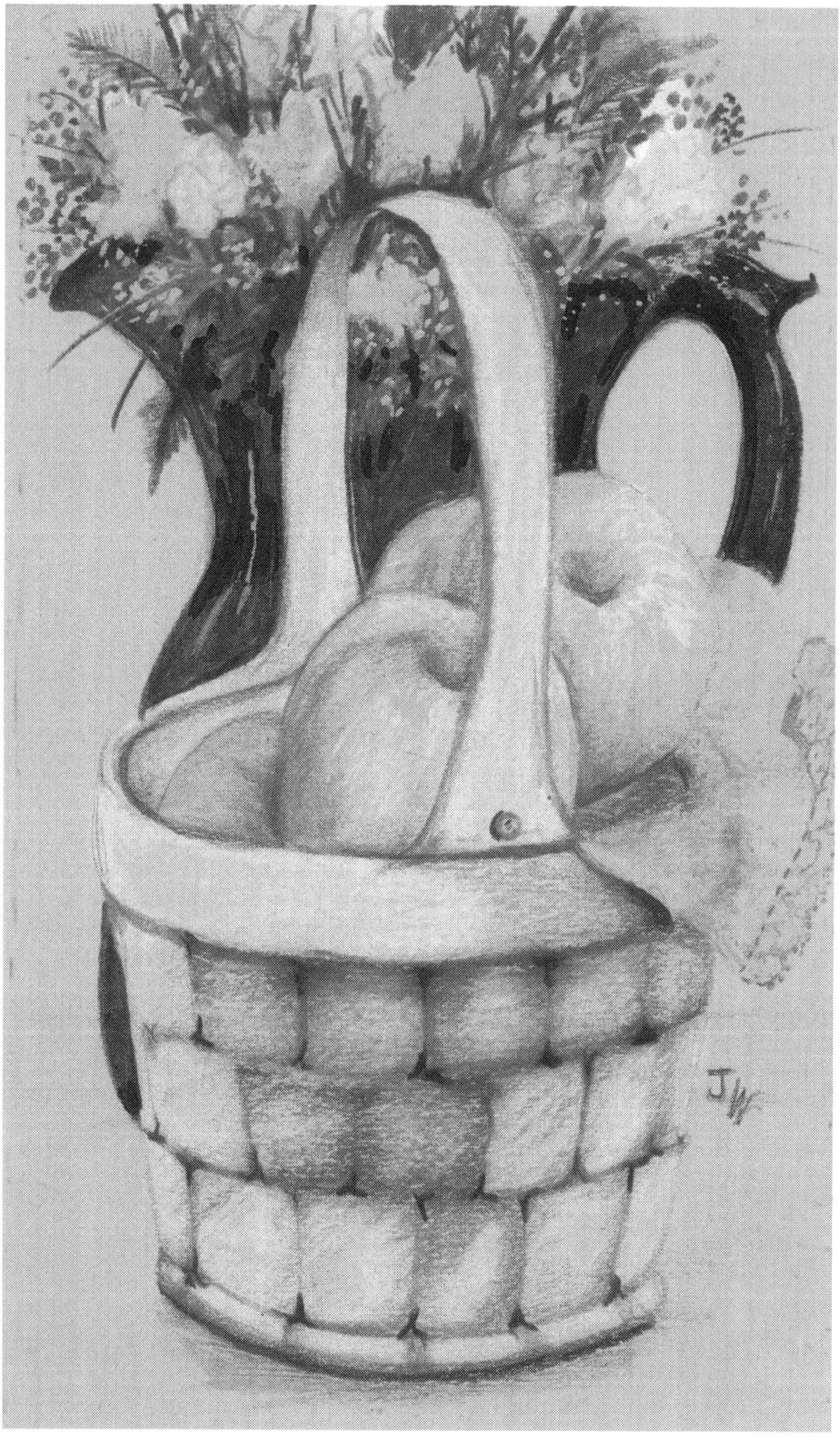

At Last, the Settlement

*"Silence is a sign of contentment...
or resignation."*

Indeed came the day when the divorce settlement finally arrived. It had taken nearly five years.

Considering the first home had been his before they married, the settlement after the second home was finally sold seemed small in comparison. Perhaps this was due to the fact that, on top of all the other problems, good legal representation had evaded him.

Still, the amount was enough to purchase a modest home. He could finally stop living like a vagabond.

The unhappy marriage had lasted for twenty-two years, and it had taken another five years for its official end to materialize. The bitter aftermath, however, would remain with him for a long time.

Perhaps what got Saint Pellicer through this devastating period was his early training. Nothing could take away or diminish an ingrained lifetime of class and dignity. He would emerge with his usual style and grace intact.

His ability to articulate his thoughts and frustrations on paper surely contributed to the therapeutic healing.

A New Beginning

"Keep your mind occupied.
It will not know when to be unhappy."

At the bottom rung on a ladder, the only direction to go is up. For Saint Pellicer, life seemed to have turned the corner for the better.

Before long, he settled into a newly-built condominium situated deeper into the sprawling suburbs. Ironically, his new home was even further away from the first home in Clayton he had not wanted to leave.

The agonizing difficulties of the past eventually began to fade as he reacquainted himself with the pleasures of once again living in comfortable surroundings.

Looking Through The Blind

Alone, standing, looking through the blind,
moving bright lights active into the night.
People, buses, cars with destination
while I am here with anticipation.
Beep, number to call, is welcome cue.
Someone caring will come to my rescue.

I Wanted More

With a fireplace in the living room,
I could not stay all day;
there was more to do
than watching those jumping flames.
I wanted more.

I decided to have in the bedroom
a black stove with logs.
There, I could stay all night
asleep, not seeing a thing.
I wanted more.

Taking a bath would be grand
with logs flaming, dancing,
peaking high, then burning low.
I put the black stove in the bathroom.
I wanted more.

I turned the lights out,
two candles flickering in the dark.
The gushing warm water filled the tub.
I turned the Jacuzzi on to soothe my soak.
I wanted more.

An hour passed, sipping a drink,
letting the flames dance over the logs,
the waters jetting, slapping my skin.
I felt refreshed and anew.
I wanted more.

My softened skin could have it no more;
it started to wrinkle, and begged a reprieve.
I stood up, wrapped in Egyptian cotton,
a towel that the pharaohs would have expected.
A flick of a switch, then a pull of the drain
ended it all.

Human experience teaches that the agonies of the past are all too soon replaced with the mundane annoyances of the present. As the adage goes, "How quickly we forget!" Condo living, for all of its pleasures and conveniences, also had its nuisances.

Unaccustomed to the close proximity of neighbors, new challenges presented themselves as Saint Pellicer learned to balance this new density with the isolation of the past.

Surrounded By Parasites

Here I am above the matron who opens and closes her blinds.
Here I am across from the bored woman with binoculars
who peeks through her blinds.
Here I am in front of the telephoto camera pointing my way.
Here I am with the jogger at midnight
stopping to see if my car has made it in for the night.
Here I am where I am told some neighbor goes through the trash.
Here I am where my car gets tampered with, and pried open.
Here I am where the gas tank cap is ajar, and water is in the gas.
Here I am where two morons make noise at my door
and run away to make my dog bark.
Here I am where four-letter words are written
on the hood of a snow-covered car.
Here I am where strangers come by, their caps snug to their ears,
face down, not wanting to catch an eye.
Here I am, surrounded by parasites.

The Victoria Years

"Angels have no fun;
up there, no one needs to."

Something was missing. Saint Pellicer wanted to remain close to his children. But his children by now were busy with their own lives.

Daughter Suzanne Almarie was living on the East Coast. Realizing that a dog's companionship would be of comfort for her lonely father, she arranged for him to have an appointment with someone at the Humane Society. There he met a small French Poodle that he adopted and named Victoria.

Please Adopt Me

My name has not been selected yet.
Oh! I want so much to become your pet.
Your very own special, warm teddy bear
that, some day, a young heir may want to share.
In a closet corner I can keep so quiet,
and I do not require a special diet.

Now this request brings me down to my knee.
Cute, soft and beige I am. Please adopt me!

Victoria's Early Morn Stretch

It is grandiose to live each daybreak
as Summer is still with us.
This was a cool morn, not for long;
the Sun came out to warm up the earth.

I sat on a steppingstone
waiting for Victoria's morning stretch
in the welcoming damp grass.
She jumped and ran and rolled over.

She walked on the edge of the embankment
with impunity, reaching the edge
of our triangular common
toward the view of the nearby lake.

Its fountain shooting high
jets of crystal clear waters,
producing gushing and breaking sounds,
sounds refreshing to the ear.

I missed bringing out a cup of coffee;
this I do each time it is perked early.
I can then linger longer,
having a second reason to be there.

Used to staying out for a short period of time,
Victoria does enjoy the extended break.
But she will come to tell me that
it is time to go in for her morning meal.

She then meanders on top of the railroad ties
that hold the ground and bushes used as a floral barrier.
Narrow paths are to her liking. Her balance is impeccable.
She maneuvers at a fast clip.

I rejoice watching her with her set habits,
her expected reaction when some canine comes by
down in the embankment.
She voicefully greets him, her tail waving.

There, at the edge of the wall,
she knows she cannot get further.
She is happier when neighbors bring by their pets
to say hello on level ground.

This is Victoria's early morn stretch.

Retreating Under The Couch

For a week and a half I have traveled
from one state to the other, frazzled;
from my home to a motel, then away
to a townhouse, now to Chesapeake Bay.

By now, a day and a half of tumult;
I have been chased, tramped on. What an insult!
Serenaded by a gauche Lab puppy,
through all of this I have remained haughty.

What is wrong to want to be left alone,
playfully enjoy the rain on my own
and run into the fields to the shoreline,
then patiently await for the sunshine?

The olive green Land Rover just pulled out.
No more Yellow Lab to hold out.
Fine, I am retreating under the couch,
for I need quiet, and to stop being a grouch.

Under The Grand Oak Tree

Under the grand oak tree the low branches
hang, swing and let in a sky that blushes
a faint rosy-blue, then gradually pale.
To hold onto daylight, it will soon fail.

I sit under. The branches brush my face,
my body leaning back against the chaise.
Victoria holds herself straight to the breeze.
Much like me, she wants this moment to seize.

The daring breeze flows between her ears;
she hears the wind and the bark of her peers.
On the alert she never lets down her guard
of what is near and away from the yard.

In the cool evening two walkers pass.
She barks, telling them, "You walk on my grass!"
I shout out, "Don't worry, she is all right;
she is friendly, do let go of your fright!"

Sitting In The Sun

The moment the door is open,
out in the Sun I have chosen
a high spot to sit and warm up,
where sounds are easy to pick up.

How wonderfully green and wide
is the land, nothing here can hide;
for soon I will let out a bark
I could stand guard until comes dark.

Sitting in the sun at the shore
can never, ever, be a bore.

When I am taken to the shore,
on the pier I stand on all four;
looking at the white sailing boat,
I dream that I would like to float.

Yes, I would like to stay right here;
this land is now so very dear,
where I can run after the fawn,
lost and bouncing in the back lawn.

Sitting in the sun at the shore
can never, ever, be a bore.

White Snow Slush

The snow started early evening and went on all night.
Now, mid-morning, nature was covered white and bright.
Victoria ran down the steps, around the corner, to the side,
jumping into the deep snow cover as if to hide.

Against the snow her coat was no more true white.
It was now champagne in the early daylight.
She jumped to move forward much like a rabbit,
the cold and the fluffy powder lifting her spirit.

Without a doubt, it was fun, for she would not stop.
Here, there and everywhere she went hop, hop and hop.
She sat for a rest, she took a taste of the white slush.
Again, again, and again she did; there was no need to rush.

Time came to return to her warm spot by the fireplace.
I brought a towel to wipe her dry, as she stood up with grace.
Her curly coat was covered with interwoven ice.
Victoria, licking my hand, my care for her was nice.

Out In The Rain

The rain was pelting the sidewalk;
it poured right and left.
Yes, I wanted to go out in the rain
to walk in puddles and get my hair wet.

The thunder did not scare me.
The lightning bypassed me.

The air was cleaned by the douse,
trails of scents were now obvious.
I followed them to know who has been there,
some friends, or someone just moved in?

The thunder did not scare me.
The lightning bypassed me.

I ignored that my master was drenched.
It is not every day I get out in the rain.
I took my time in this adventure.
I scouted and sniffed and jumped for more.

The thunder did not scare me.
The lightning bypassed me.

I always anticipate the warmth of the fire,
the towel that will rub me dry,
the care that is there to get
when one is such good company as a French Poodle!

The thunder did not scare me.
The lightning bypassed me.
My master was drenched.
I scouted and sniffed and jumped for more.

Many happy years would pass before Victoria would be laid to rest, appropriately, in a Victorian garden at the home of friends. She would never be forgotten.

I Must Let You Go

I love you so and want to hold you tight,
as your life is getting less bright.
You are aging; now you are past eighty.
So far, your strength has been mighty.

The vet prescribed pills that stopped to work;
each time you take them you say, "Irk!"
You lose the water that your body retains
and immediately get it back, once it drains.

You stayed in the hospital for intensive care.
I am told there is no repair.
They want to see that you end quietly
for a deserved rest without agony.

For me to hold on with a thinning rope
to your love and more days of hope
is egotistical, for it only prolongs what will come.
Fond memories will become an endless poem.

You have brought happiness to my aging climb;
I am also reaching that time.
You were playful, jumping high in the snow;
this is the way I will remember the Victoria I know.

Farewell with love.
I must let you go.

Memories of the Eastern Shore

"The infatuation of the moment does not let us face up to reality."

A special time of year for Saint Pellicer was his annual trek to his daughter's vacation getaway on the Eastern Shore. Suzanne Almarie, an enterprising young woman, had acquired a second property at a time when many of her contemporaries were still renting apartments.

Each summer he and Victoria would leave Saint Louis behind for a few weeks and settle into Suzanne's charming cottage known as Au bord de l'eau, situated near the Chesapeake Bay.

Au bord de l'eau

Au bord de l'eau
at the water's edge
my love remains.

Au bord de l'eau
at the water's edge
au revoir with pains.

I think of you,
lost without you
so miserable.

I think of you,
lost without you
left insatiable.

I Am The Waterman

I am the waterman of Chesapeake Bay.
I am the waterman out every day.
Third generation catching the crabs to stay,
my son will follow tradition some day.

With a sweatshirt under my rubber suit,
with heavy rubber hat and rubber boot,
through the fog I leave early in the dark,
even before the young dogs get to bark.

I am the waterman of Chesapeake Bay.
I am the waterman out every day.

I let the ropes of my boat from the pier,
slowly get the motor started to steer,
to engage the white boat toward the wide bay,
when the skies are still painted of dark grey.

The waters may be rough or may be cold;
nothing will put the morning sail on hold.
The lines with bait are set to buoy pointers,
then dragged with chains getting early crawlers.

I am the waterman of Chesapeake Bay.
I am the waterman out every day.

Most are good days with many a bushel
of crabs crowded, and of crabs that twiddle.
On the wooden pier's scale they weigh for pay;
in iced trucks, to the market they're on their way.

I am the waterman of Chesapeake Bay.
I am the waterman out every day.
The waterman with the girl down the way,
the waterman going my father's way.

WINE
J Wolff

Autumn

*"My life is of chapters,
each one with its own title."*

Autumn, A Clean Sweep

*Summer drew the sieve, left leaves beat,
forceful, drenched the hard ground with heat,
lanced sun rays to fruit, ripe to death,
stiff, it stood until the last breath.
Summer, the end.*

*Fighting, Autumn brought a slow stop,
thunder, rain and wind, a temp drop;
to the grass, a new spur of green.
Reprieve, a new life with a sheen.
Autumn, green, a reprieve.*

*Compassion left everything moist,
taking over, the drought to foist;
blushing of color, gradual,
a panorama provincial.
Autumn, aging beauty.*

*Infernal heat gone, livable;
morning earth in mist, lyrical.
Across land, the winds blow and weep,
pushing twigs and leaves, a clean sweep.
Autumn, pushing clean.*

Balmar Farm

Hidden in the woods not far from the road
is Balmar Farm. You can hear a happy toad
at the bank, ready to leap into the pond
for a quick lunch of insects, aiming beyond.

Golden Retriever runs near to the wood,
chasing a rabbit, gone from where he stood.
Undisturbed deer in the forest hiding,
guests with horses through narrow trails riding.

Forceful tractor pulls a flatbed of hay
along the farm roads; visiting guests sway,
sitting and holding on the edge for a ride.
Squire recounts Balmar's history with pride.

At nightfall, near the house, burning torches;
red charcoal in pits, steaks, chicken scorches,
white smoke of hickory up the clear sky;
a breeze gentle and cool, almost too shy.

Over a country meal lifting fine wines,
debates flourish, go ripe. Much like grapevines,
they start, divided into branches, a thought
soon to reach a final outcome, well wrought.

At Balmar, centers a meeting of minds –
inquisitive, well-read, funny, all kinds.
The mysterious blend is due to its host
who could even find for his party a ghost!

Balmar Farm

Bill Ballard

"Rejoice at the diversity of your neighbors. They enrich your lives."

For Saint Pellicer, a new life was beginning at age sixty. He gradually began to surround himself with new acquaintances intrigued with his artistic if somewhat eccentric nature, who would become instrumental in helping him achieve his creative goals.

An evening at a fundraiser at the Loretto Hilton Theatre produced one of the first of these new acquaintances. Bill Ballard, long a patron of the arts, noticed Saint Pellicer's stately manner and quickly learned that he was a writer and a poet.

Ballard became instrumental in helping Saint Pellicer reestablish himself after the painful years following his divorce. Thus began a long friendship that included many hours at Ballard's Balmar Farm, his sprawling e[illegible]

Marcel Toussaint

"Poetry must be an adventure today,
remembering the past recording for tomorrow."

A rebirth of his artistic past had emerged. Saint Pellicer wanted to choose a name that he could use professionally for his writing. One chapter had ended, and a new one was starting. A professional name would help him achieve his goal of a fresh start on his life.

During childhood, his closest friend had been a boy named Marcel. And because Saint Pellicer had been born on All Saints Day, his father had given him the sobriquet of *Toussaint* at birth. "Marcel Toussaint" seemed the logical choice because it would make him feel connected to his past.

Emil Stanley Saint Pellicer, writer, poet, actor, soldier, dance master, teacher of deportment, fencing master, administrator, husband and father, was now also Marcel Toussaint.

A Lone Voyager

In this life, I am a lone voyager
in this world to become a raconteur
of events, people, lost love and the like;
to write, to read, to perform at the mike.

Of emotions I make a short story,
from the heart, seldom ends up in glory,
often sad as my audience wants to cry
when of torment, my characters do sigh.

I came without knowledge, without a thing,
without a Winter, and without a spring,
influenced by Autumn, dried by Summer,
bewildered and curious, a newcomer.

I have learned to cry, to shout and to laugh,
to experience the whole, never a half,
to look for happiness whenever sad,
and write everything on my yellow pad.

Time came to forget my father could sing;
for silent I have stayed, feeling the sting.
It is time to try my voice, sing in a show;
to rejoice with verses that often flow.

Her Looks Got Your Attention

She was petite, somewhat fragile,
here and there on the stage, so mobile;
quick to be prepared – her makeup perfect,
her blond hair sparkling, a white gown for effect.

Her high heels gave her silhouette an uplift,
nothing in her presence was to go adrift.
She portrayed a daring presence,
a calculated elegance with affluence.

Front center, with her guitar on stage,
her melodious voice kept with the musical page,
tender in the caring moments,
firm and assertive in the vigorous fragments.

She put all of herself into her voice and music
with equal passion to entertain the public.
Her favorite numbers were attention-getting,
always with a stage aplomb befitting.

To love her music was easy, her five-man band
electrified musically the grandstand,
projecting deep into the audience
melodies to achieve a memorable ambiance.

Yes, her looks got your attention,
then her singing got you with emotion;
the music got you quietly singing
all along with your feet on the floor tapping.

The Bluegrass Connection

Christine Peick

"The perceptions and beauty of one art form bleed into another."

Toussaint was mulling over the possibility of pursuing something he had inherited from his father: a love for singing. The intimidation he had felt as a child when comparing himself with his father had never disappeared.

Meanwhile, the singer Christine Peick had recently organized Raven Moon, a group of Bluegrass musicians. She would frequently play guitar and sing at The Focal Point.

Just down the street was a coffee shop called Pony Espresso. Here, Toussaint would often read his poetry. In time their paths crossed – he, interested in the music at The Focal Point; she, after a performance, craving some refreshment during a poetry session.

Christine was perfecting her voice and, in conversation over coffee, discovered that Toussaint, too, was interested in exploring his own possibilities. In time, she introduced him to her voice coach, known as the Directress. Toussaint and Christine became friends, and would meet after the shows organized by the Directress. The two delivered positive feedback to each other, and bolstered mutual self-confidence.

The Directress, or the *Direct-Stress*, as she soon became known, had her own ideas of singing and performance that interfered with Toussaint's perceptions. Although they sometimes clashed, for a while he persevered. In time, the stress became too intense, and his relationship with the Directress came to an end.

The friendship with Christine, however, was for life.

Toussaint became an occasional guest of Christine and her husband, Bill, at their elegant home surrounded by beautiful gardens and woodland.

Elsie Parker and The Poor People of Paris

"To be creative often requires ignoring what has already been done."

In the mid-nineties, a group called The Poor People of Paris came to Toussaint's attention. The group, two talented women, Elsie Parker and Donita Bauer, performed French music at Brandt's Café.

Some years earlier, our good friends Rusty and Mark Werner "discovered" this group one summer evening as they were visiting the University City entertainment district. They immediately became admirers of their music and suggested that we listen to this talented duo. By the time Toussaint arrived on the scene, the Werners and we had already become long-time fans.

The French poet established a rapport with the singer and her keyboard accompanist, and the possibility of setting his lyrics to music became a reality. Among the achievements that came about were the recordings of two songs for which Elsie Parker and Donita Bauer collaborated on the music and Toussaint wrote the lyrics – *Elle se souvient,* which became the title song for The Poor People of Paris's first CD in 1997, and *La poule de Pigalle,* which was included in their second CD in 2001. Both songs were eventually set to orchestration.

In Year 2000, The Bob Coleman Orchestra, together with The Poor People of Paris, performed *Elle se souvient* at Powell Hall in a concert entitled *April in Paris*. *La poule de Pigalle* would premier as an orchestration in 2005.

Wayne Coniglio would miss this premier by one year. A talented musician who had traveled Europe for eight years as a trombonist with Ray Charles, Coniglio would eventually become part of The Poor People of Paris, filling multiple roles as bassist, trombonist and arranger – and a supporter of Toussaint's poetic and lyrical endeavors.

She Remembers

(Elle se souvient)

Of her lovers she has made a list
writing crève coeur poems, austere,
she lives miserable, so exacting,
so young at sixteen, her heart with gloom.

With despair always,
when each love seems lost .

At night she walks the avenue
shadow projected on walls, headlights passing
at the wheels, guys, powerful sudden stops,
without emotions, a false ingenue.

Heart broken always,
the nights are for love.

With great despair, she looks for a sweet word,
a sincere caress, a love she has lost,
believing it is just there at each encounter.
It is her young love, not her heart she rents.

With despair always,
when each love seems lost.

A hidden place, a forest hideaway
for two, from young fright her body vibrates,
kisses covered, a handsome disturbing lover,
she remembers her first rendez-vous.

Heart broken always,
the nights are for love.

She remembers her first rendez-vous.
She remembers her first rendez-vous.
She remembers her first rendezvous.

Elle se souvient

(She Remembers)

De ses amants elle en a fait une liste
écrivant ses poèmes de coeur, austères,
elle a vécu misérable, si sévère,
c'est une jeune fille de seize ans, bien triste.

Désespoir toujours,
perdu semble l'amour.

La nuit elle se promène dans l'avenue
ombre projetée aux murs, des phares passants
au volant des gars, coups de freins puissants
sans émotion, faussement ingénue.

Coeur brisé toujours,
tous les soirs l'amour.

Au grand désespoir, elle cherche un mot doux,
caresse sincère, amour qu'elle a perdu,
craignant le moment là à chaque venue.
C'est son amour et non son coeur qu'elle loue.

Désespoir toujours,
perdu semble l'amour.

Une cache dans la forêt, un trou-de-loup
bien a deux, d'une jeune peur son corps vibrant
baisers partout, un bel amant troublant
elle se souvient du premier rendez-vous.

Coeur brisé toujours,
tous les soirs l'amour.

Elle se souvient du premier rendez-vous.
Elle se souvient du premier rendez-vous.
Elle se souvient du premier rendez-vous.

The Hen Of Pigalle

(La poule de Pigalle)

She is a "lady of the night," walking
the luminous sidewalks of Pigalle,
paying no attention to her rivals,
late, as the night gets settled, dancing.

Her makeup is very theatrical,
provoking, bright red accents on cheeks,
mascara weighing eyelashes down to tips,
her face veiling all ancestral traits.

The poule of Pigalle,
without a rival,
luxuriously dressed
with fur for feathers.

Her bleached hair hides her age,
her lips painted in ghastly style,
coated with a waxy purple,
a woman not wanting to be wise.

Lustrous, her hair, curly, falls
over dark coat, its collar of mink.
Her sad portrait held captive
in a heavy beret of faded felt.

She is a "lady of the night," walking
the luminous sidewalks of Pigalle,
paying no attention to her rivals,
late, as the night gets settled, dancing.

The hen of of Pigalle,
without a rival,
luxuriously dressed
with furs for feathers.

La poule de Pigalle

(The Hen Of Pigalle)

C'est une poule de luxe, marchant
Les trottoirs lumineux de Pigalle,
sans prendre compte des ses rivales
tard, lorsque la nuit s'installe en dansant.

Son maquillage est bien théâtral,
provoquant, accents rouge vifs sur joues,
mascara pesant les cils jusqu'aux bouts,
son visage voile tout trait ancestral.

C'est la poule de Pigalle,
toujours sans rivale,
de luxe en parure,
plumes et fourrure.

Cheveux oxygénés cachent l'âge
ses lèvres peintes au style fauve
couvertes de cire couleur mauve,
de femme ne voulant être sage.

Reluisant ses cheveux tombent arqués
sur manteau noir au col de vison
son portrait grotesque est en prison
dans un lourd béret de feutre fané.

C'est une poule de luxe, marchant
les trottoirs lumineux de Pigalle,
sans prendre compte des ses rivales
tard, lorsque la nuit s'installe en dansant.

C'est la poule de Pigalle,
toujours sans rivale,
de luxe en parure,
plumes et fourrure.

Benton Park

*"If you read my English poetry you will speak French in a year…
At least you will have a window into
the thoughts of a Frenchman …"*

Through French Doors

*Sitting on the bench in the hallway,
looking through the French doors
is like watching a live screen play
that will end up in our memoirs.*

*To sit in the room with them is not the same;
each door panel has its own framed portrait.
The burning wood logs have a brighter flame;
you focus on each individual trait.*

*It is much like panning with a camera
for a silent film with no words to hear.
You must imagine a fitting drama
happening in episodes live, so near.*

*Sitting on the bench in the hallway,
looking through the French doors
is like watching a live screen play
that will end up in our memoirs.*

In the mid to late nineties, Charlie and I began to notice the bright, if sometimes edgy demeanor of the engaging, rather eccentric Frenchman who could often be found at The Poor People of Paris performances. At first, conversation among us was usually limited to cordial greetings.

During breaks, it was amusing to observe how quickly he could evolve from an audience participant into a successful salesman, selling their CDs. Then one evening, Toussaint politely requested of Charlie if he could ask me to dance. Although a bit taken aback, I accepted, and the friendship eventually flourished. Years later, we would discover that Elsie Parker had initially suggested that Toussaint see about having me as a dance partner.

We began to entertain The Poor People of Paris and Toussaint regularly at our City home in Benton Park, following various performances.

In year 2000, we hosted a reception following the *April in Paris* concert at Powell Hall and encouraged Toussaint and The Poor People of Paris to invite guests attending the concert to the reception. There, we met his friends, Bill Ballard and Christine Peick. That evening, old and new friendships began to intertwine, forming an artistic tapestry destined to last a lifetime.

Absolutely!

To be alive requires a celebration
when the doc gives you his affirmation
that all is well and the shining sun is yours,
and the future has many more encores.

You gathered your friends, oh what a crowd,
the ones that make you so proud.
You lavished them with a sumptuous party
in your elegant retreat so classy.

They came for an impromptu celebration,
with well-deserved appreciation.
They suggested you make this gathering yearly.
You smiled and said, "Absolutely!"

Cabaret In Benton Park

Our hosts wanted to end the year with a flourish
and start the new one with hope,
once again gathering friends, musicians and singers
who had graced their ears for years.

Linda and Charlie Dahlheimer transformed their manse
into a Cabaret of the fifties with decorative flair;
the grand piano, majestic in the living room,
where important performers have sat on the bench.

The well-chosen audience responded
with delight to the invite
to come for a sumptuous dinner,
appreciate the excellent wines, the fine desserts.

They sat in the adjoining dining room
turned into a bar and buffet service;
candles of many heights lit for ambiance.
Here, elegance was at the forefront.

Jim Kreisman sparkled with his entertaining music,
fingers rolling over the keys
gliding into crescendos,
plunging into the composers' notes with gusto.

Rusty LaDon, of the Moskus In Exile era,
revived her well-known successes,
a voice that is as clear and modulated
as in those long-ago days of "God Bless The Child."

Jan Mahannah of Gaslight Square fame
sang from her nightclub repertoire
show tunes and spirited ballads,
with a style that resonated.

Alan Appt, an admirer of Frank Sinatra,
entertained vibrantly with "I've Got You Under My Skin,"
bold in his imitations of the singer
he admires so much.

Elsie Parker, of The Poor People of Paris,
shined in "La vie en rose" of Edith Piaf,
"One at a Time" from Michel le Grand,
"Elle se souvient," lyrics, Marcel Toussaint.

Marcel Toussaint reached into his past
with "Je suis seul ce soir" of Charles Trenet
whom he admired in his younger years
as an adolescent Frenchman.

Mark Werner with his cigar box guitar
plucked the strings, to our surprise with finesse;
singing along with amusing lyrics,
bringing some smiles from the audience.

At the bass was Wayne Coniglio,
stringing supportive notes to the subtle
selections of a fun evening,
giving dimension to a piano-bass association.

Ron Reichard, in true Bing Crosby style,
took the enchanted guests back
to a nostalgic place in time,
his rich voice complementing his gentle guitar.

Ever the reluctant virtuoso, Michael, at midnight,
seated himself at the piano, his body upright.
The audience, assured this time he would perform,
waited, mesmerized, for the magic to begin.

At the end of the evening we all bade farewell
to the old year,
starting the New Year with cheers,
hugs, good wishes – and a toast of champagne.

An Orchestral Arrangement

In time, my husband and I felt it would be fun to see about having an orchestration created for a song for which Marcel Toussaint had written the lyrics, and The Poor People of Paris, the music. *La poule de Pigalle* had been written several years earlier, and seemed a fine candidate. We liked the words, we liked the music and, possibly most importantly, we liked its creators.

The orchestration premiered at a concert at Southern Illinois University Carbondale in 2005, as Elsie Parker performed *La poule de Pigalle*, accompanied by the university orchestra.

The Arrangement

To write lyrics is what I like most,
and, then, they have to find a host:
a composer inspired by the words,
a singer who can sound out the chords.

Planned are performances with hopes of success.
Meanwhile, time idles through the long process.
Ahead is the hope of a professional recording
on a CD that is destined for a smart marketing.

Requests for the song soon grow.
The demands for the CD now flow.
Comes the time of need for a new issue
for the happy artists next to pursue.

All is well, we tell ourselves, but then,
for an arranger, we will need the pen.
The composer finds a competent mind;
the right musical talent is quite a find.

Next on the agenda, a patron of the arts,
one who will support our financial parts.
Ahead was a vision this may be possible;
reaching the goal would seem celestial.

While the possibility of an arrangement rambled,
a symphony would play it; we liked the gamble.
We discussed it with our friends as fact;
unknowingly, there would come a pact.

Linda mentioned that, "Charlie and I should;
and, as aficionados of French music, we would."
They liked the music, and word rhythms of each verse.
The "Arrangement" became the piece to rehearse.

The moment in the elegant Shryock Auditorium had come;
The Poor People of Paris, so memorably awesome;
the Southern Illinois Symphony, so sensational;
Elsie Parker singing La poule de Pigalle, so emotional.

It took the participation of many an artist;
the song was a hit — not a mere name on a list.
And were it not for Linda and Charlie,
"The Arrangement" would never now be.

Life Is a Cabaret

The author has enjoyed a rich social life for many years. No stranger to a microphone, Toussaint's participation in poetry events fostered many friendships. He could also be counted on to be an enthusiastic part of the audience – at cabarets, clubs, hotel lobbies, restaurants, theatres, concert halls, and outdoor festivals. He was drawn to these events by the promise of good times with friends – both onstage and off.

The entertainment would range from haunting French songs by Elsie Parker and The Poor People of Paris at the venerable Café de France, the nostalgic Brandt's Cafe, and the elegant lobbies of the Ritz Carlton and the Adam's Mark, to the soulful Bluegrass tunes of Christine Peick and her Raven Moon band at The Focal Point or the Schlafly Tap Room. Some nights, vocalist Curt Landes would entertain at his keyboard at Truffles; other times, Wayne Coniglio's jazzy trombone could be heard at Finale. Swing Set would set the mood one evening at The Crossing, and Farshid Etniko and its Latin rhythms at Café Eau, another. Christopher Voelker's jazz violin was equally at home in the stately halls of the Art Museum and at the bustling JaBoni nightclub. At the popular Mihalis Lounge, Gene Lynn's Frank Sinatra tunes would complement Kecia Davis's vibrant Motown.

Outdoor venues ranged from gala street parties in quaint Sainte Genevieve or historic Saint Charles, to concerts on the Washington University Quadrangle, the Botanical Gardens, or at the Muny in Forest Park. On summer evenings, Stan Fornaszewski's Big Band would deliver smooth moonlight serenades on the East Side from a city park bandstand.

The above portrayal of who performed where is a bit sketchy, since most of these musicians actually entertained at a number of these venues over time. Our home on New Year's Eve was also a destination spot, as was Dianne Meyers's carriage house in Soulard.

Fourth of July would be celebrated at the Art Deco home of the Luepkers on the scenic Mississippi bluffs. While guests awaited the Downtown fireworks extravaganza, anything could happen – from a ride in an antique electric car to the sound of steam whistles from the caliope played by Stan Kann.

These gatherings would quickly fill and, along with Toussaint, we would find ourselves surrounded with assortments of such illustrious guests as Alan and Pam Appt, Kathy Atwood and Bill Ballard, Jan Mahannah and Bob Casey, Gerry and Jean Childers, Brett Cervantes, Sylvie Esparel, Ted and Edna Gravenhorst, Jack Smiley and Mary Willis, and Mark and Rusty Werner.

The venues would come and go, but there would always be new ones to explore.

Never a passive participant, Toussaint constantly captured these events with his digital camera and with his photographic memory – keenly observing and retaining the most minute details of these fleeting moments for later transformation into enduring poetic memories.

Forgetting The Time

At dusk, candles glowed in the musical bars
to fiery guitar-picking under the stars.
There were the musicians, songwriters, singers,
and, hidden in growing darkness, the lovers.

The geese and the ducks in the lake gently glide
past a lonely fisherman at the dockside.
The half moon, envious, giving out a glow
over the summer evening unfolding below.

To cool down from their spirited renditions,
some performers quietly changed locations.
They retreated inside the main house, immersed
in finding refreshments to appease their thirst.

Festive, the evening went on past midnight,
the sounds of the strings reaching the moonlight
where guitar, banjo, bass and violin
joined in with the joyous, soft mandolin.

There Was The Rose

In the garden among the thorns
after the dew of early morns
velvet petals of red held firm,
curled as if by a human perm;
proud, elegant, there was a rose,
subject of verses and of prose.

She made it to the flower shop
away from the more common crop;
her grace took her to a tall vase,
she stood for everyone to gaze
on top of a black piano grand,
soon to be seized by a quick hand.

To the tune of French piano sounds
from the thirties, forties, old rounds,
the singer's feelings came to a crest.
She turned, took the rose with a jest.
As if it were part of her act,
the rose was taken away, with tact.

There was the rose.
Now, it is gone.

Rowdy Women

In a little town lost in the darkness of the night,
the pub was crowded in a setting of dim light.
A television on was ignored, no one interested in sports;
this was the time to play where everyone cavorts.

There was a rowdy group of women, ageless,
loud and boisterous showing off their fitness.
Their clothing clung over their curves, preserved,
which kept them packaged, as if corseted.

Their makeup was overdone, almost for stage light;
they were caricatures of theatre ladies, out for the night,
with hair tinted, each in a striking shade.
You wondered if in their garter they kept a blade.

The show was on, and quiet were the men
who stood there passive, letting it all happen.
Drinks were bought, others offered, on a make;
the men were nonchalant, waiting for their take.

The weekend ladies, in poses, flaunted their wares
to country men, tough, muscular and as big as bears.
To be noticed, the "ladies" raised their silly, shrill talk.
The men were physical; to nonsense would not flock.

Late in the night, the men became bold,
now wanting for some of the beauties to hold
in their monster trucks in the secluded countryside
with music enticing, their emotions amplified.

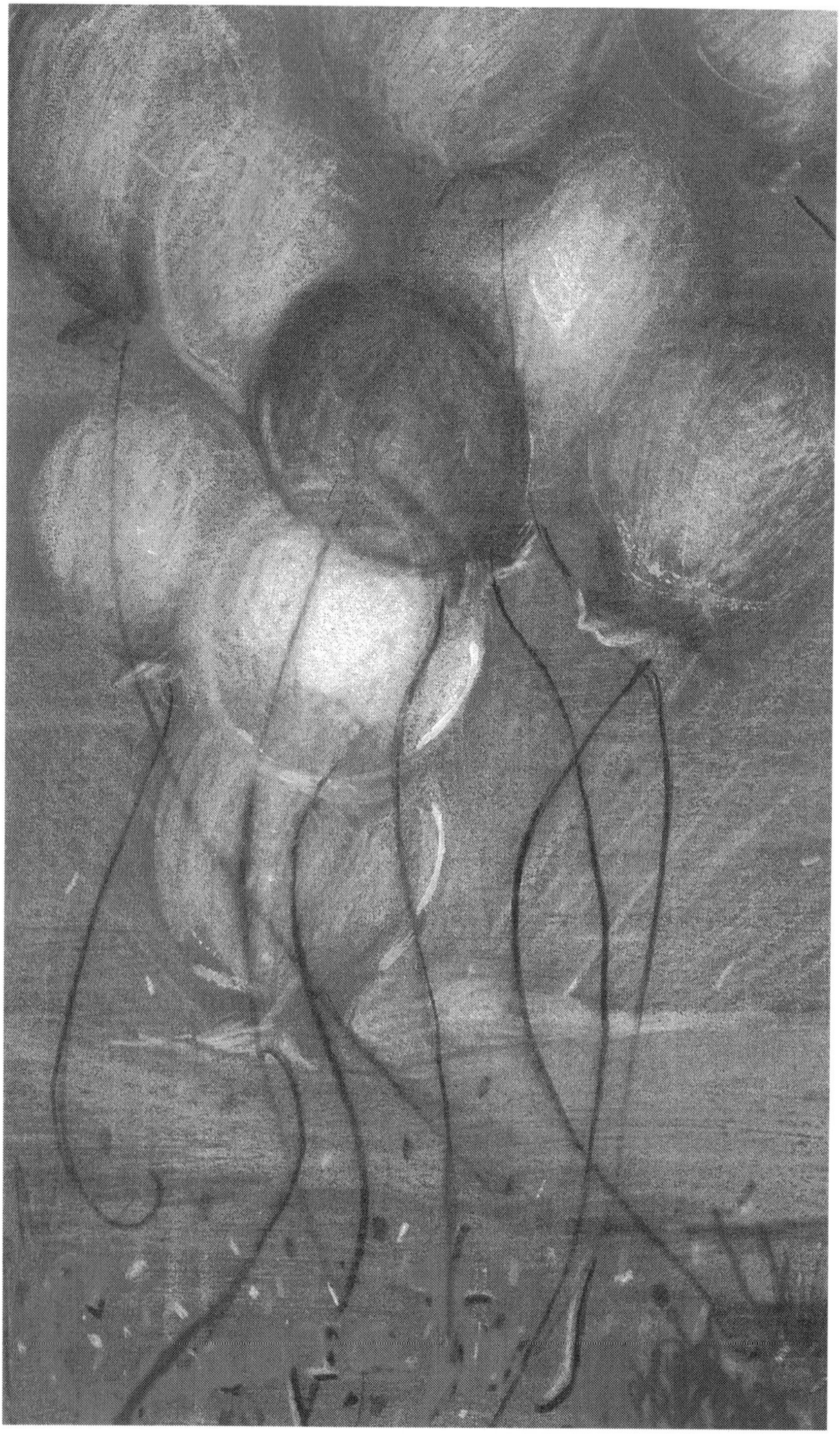

Fireworks Over The Bluffs

This was a special tradition for celebration buffs
to spend the eve of the Fourth just over the bluffs.
From the Luepker's house sitting near to the edge,
its terraces inviting to come close to the ledge.

The banks, sparkling with lights on both sides of the river,
provided a peaceful haven for a grand life of leisure.
Away from these heights just south of Downtown
the Arch shined, in its brilliance, right at sundown.

The seventy guests clustered at round tables,
delighted in dinner, outside, just under the gables.
Time arrived for the fireworks show in the distance;
an acrobatic plane flew, delighting the audience.

It spread colored sparkles and bright swerving curves
that followed its path, deftly avoiding the swerves.
The elaborate bursts delighted those at the Fair,
colorful, powerful, grandiose, then an end with a flair.

Another celebration had passed, just south of this City,
steeped, first, in French history, and now, American glory.
Grateful to Sue and Marty, and with many warm thanks
it was time to leave these enchanting riverbanks.

Bravo As Ever

While the sun was not out,
the skies were overtaken by a light intermittent rain.
It was a pleasure to admire the garden blooming,
the trees with branches covered with leaves,
the greenest of banks,
the rippling lake.
The male mallards were playing fearlessly
among themselves,
vibrant, daring,
at a start of a Spring still young.
Nature was nurturing its domain
with the attention of a doting mother.

The chimenea radiated the very comforting warmth
of a log-burning fire.
Bill was very attentive to see
that the flames would get plenty wood
to spark and spread
in the confines of the creative outdoor stove.

Christine orchestrated the garden party.
An accomplished hostess,
she had invited a company delightful, talkative,
with amusing sayings and stories
that did make us laugh much more than usual.
This was a perfect remedy to lift up
spirits worn out from a long week of obligations,
far from the hustle of city environs,
in a paradise of elegant living
and the serenity of the country.

Bravo, as ever.

The Official Poet

"A poet cannot be just a reporter but an artist who paints with words."

Long a writer of poetry, Toussaint published his first poetry booklet, *Remember Me Young*, in the nineties. He has been invited to read at various venues, including National Public Radio, and his poems have been featured in fourteen anthologies, including *America At The Millennium*.

Poetry Mentor

Aaron Belz, teacher, poetry promoteur extraordinaire, and moderator of Observable Readings at the Modern Arts Museum in Saint Louis, contacted Toussaint, whom he described as "that mysterious man," for a possible reading. This eventually led to a meeting, an interview, and ultimately an invitation to read at Observable Readings at the museum, a classy event that the poet enjoyed tremendously. Belz suggested that Toussaint join the Saint Louis Writers Guild for channeling his poetry interest – a suggestion that he found most rewarding.

The Muse Follows

The muse follows
around,
while driving
just did,
over grocery tickets
I write,
paper on the wheel,
steering.

The muse never waits
to see
if paper, pencil
are nearby
to record
a good thought
at the worst of times.

On Poetry

Poetry is an adventure
of stimulating thoughts
inscribed to last on paper
in calculated lines
with words chosen carefully,
ending with rhymes or not.

Poetry is more satisfying
than crossword puzzles,
for you can use your own words
rather than discover
someone else's verbiage.

For poetry to be obscure
is a grave mistake;
it should not be a mystery of thoughts
but rather an inspiring work
with a perception that is clear.

Poetry should not be an accumulation
of overwhelming abstruse words;
they reveal a poet who went to great length
to discover them, to often misuse them.

Poetry that is only a reflection
of daily conversation is not poetry.
Poetry, like music, should have a certain élan
in the construction of its phrasing.

I refuse to read poetry that irritates me
with a language bland, or overly pompous,
an irrelevant message,
absent of a unifying reflection.

Poetry must be a pleasure to read,
not an obstacle course of ill-cast thoughts.

A Day at the VA

*"People who have a notion of who they are
radiate self-acceptance
and tolerance toward others."*

Toussaint entered a competition in the 2009 National Veterans Creative Arts Program. Charlie and I were on hand that evening to cheer him on, along with Alan and Pam Appt, Rusty and Mark Werner, Christine Peick, his niece Odette Carter Kaufman and her husband, Rick. His efforts initially earned him not one, but three gold medal awards at the local level:

1) Poetry Patriotic: *Today is a Great Day*
2) Poetry Personal Humorous: *The Senior Veteran Beach Boy Contest*
3) Photography Portrait: *Faces of Honor – A Portrait of an Honor Guard*

An avid photographer, Toussaint has delighted many of his friends, capturing events on camera for posterity. It is not unusual for him to capture over one hundred photos in one evening.

Months later, competing with hundreds of entries from across the nation, *The Senior Veteran Beach Boy Contest* won the national Second Place award. Toussaint immediately began preparing for the next year's competition, hoping to become eligible to participate in the annual gala variety show.

The Kudos Continue

The poet recently won an award for two poems at the St. Louis Writers Guild's Poetry Throwdown at the Focal Point: the decadent *She Drives A Red Convertible* and the dark *Observing From The Corner.* Judging was based on both content and delivery. Only two of the other twenty-two contestants exceeded him in awards.

Over the years, he has frequently been heard reading his poetry at various cafés, clubs, art centers, museums and bookstores.

With his flair for writing poetry, Toussaint writes not only on a variety of topics, but also about the creation and the delivery of the poetry itself.

Today Is A Great Day

The sun is memorable
lifting above the horizon
wanting to reach the apogee
of a historical moment in the making.

Change is what we have been wanting.
We celebrate with anticipation
a tomorrow with a new beginning
of hope and healing of a nation.

It took a man with a vision
daring to be himself,
with strong character and compassion
to show courage during elections.

He rallied the broken spirits
of our weary people, putting
the diverging parts into one ideal,
a unique vision of America of the future.

Eloquence is his powerful media,
his towering stature impressive,
his intellect evident,
inquisitive, analytic, solving.

He knows how to mediate
intolerance with inflexible demands,
showing how we will all gain,
guided by reason, kindness and a good heart.

He is Barack Obama,
President
of these United States

(*Today is a Great Day* will be printed in the National Veterans *Poetry Anthology* of 2009.)

The Senior Veteran Beach Boy Contest

A VA Doctor monitoring my heart
prescribed an exercise program
after a cardiac arrest. A pacemaker
and defibrillator were implanted in my chest.

I was not ready for such regiment.
Wanting to get to the program,
I worked a slow recovery at my own pace.
It was obvious; guided supervision was a must.

A year went by, my strength now better,
still my knee troubled me at each step.
I tried a cane and this helped some.
I decided to go to Paris to read poetry.

My reading was grand among Paris talents.
I felt as if young again. with my French accent,
could not get used to being called "the American"
when introduced at the microphone.

In Paris, a walk is a long walk—
steps mean hundreds of them,
up and down the Metro, down to the riverboats,
to museums and public gardens.

This was the everyday physical stress
that I endured with pain and not a word.
To me, Paris was not the Eiffel Tower.
Paris was endless with up and down steps.

Coming back home to face
ten or so steps up my condo
was nothing to pain about anymore,
for Paris was tougher with the most.

I went to see the VA Doctor.
He knew this time was right to start
the exercise program that I had snubbed.
He assigned me at the gym a medical trainer.

Twice a week I walk, cycle, use building machines.
I have learnt to perspire - somewhat,
increase the weights for meaningful resistance.
Three months - and the results are there!

My chest muscles have new shapes;
my arms are no more of the matchstick kind.
My legs are firm, my knees better,
my breathing is like that of a younger man.

I feel so grand! My defibrillator at peace,
the pacemaker humming when in need,
my memory sharpened with a wont to write,
a renewed life with a prolonged future.

At seventy-six, I finally have
what never before worked out --
a body sculptured with definition. Should I enter
the Senior Veteran Beach Boy Contest?

A Vintage Evening

The background of a full restaurant of diners enjoying themselves relaxed by the free flowing of wine tells a tale of lively conversations. The music of decades ago from a resplendent Paris, with songs that still have meaning today, was a few decibels over this humming background noise.

Everyone was happily relaxed, wanting to participate in the exuberance of the singer who became more "French" as her intermittent sips of red wine were more closely savored. Her facial expressions, her expressive physical body and arms reflecting each mood launched by the songs, encouraged the listening admirers to become vocal about her performance. The pianist, for the first time seen having a glass of Beaujolais Nouveau, played with more emphatic fingers over the vibrating keyboard.

After dinner, many lingered for conversation with the artists and purchased the CDs that would at home recreate the French mood of cabaret singing they had just applauded with enthusiasm. The fancy tip jar had been graciously filled with bills by the most enthused, who wanted to say thanks for a grand time. The Poor People of Paris, as American as the members are, sounded and looked as Parisian as one can be in Saint Louis in the very center of the sedate Midwest. The café, with its updated decor of vibrant colors and its ambiance, seemed European. The subdued micro spotlights blended the quaint place into a cabaret.

The Beaujolais Nouveau was a fine reason for creating a most successful gathering.

The Countryside

"Colors affect your mood."

Bill Ballard's …

Owl Creek Farm

Some tree leaves turning to yellow and rust,
discreet color this time of year, a bust
of an early fall wanting to stay warm.
An Indian Summer, a Midwestern norm.

It was uphill, downhill, curves to the right,
curves to the left, a fairly high speed fright,
a road toboggan reaching through landmarks,
through knoll, then hills at the foot of the Ozarks.

We reached Caledonia, then Owl Creek Farm.
Leonard Hall once owned this Possum Trot Farm.
He fondly described it in writing so great,
guardian of history is a side gate.

The tall grasses in the prairie were dense,
forming a rugged continuous fence.
We walked in file, the leader cutting trail
with gear moving ahead as fast as a snail.

Two creeks meandering into a third;
the water, crystal clear, seemed still in gird
through bluffs and hills in a picturesque course,
hiding its vigor, coming from the source.

We sat, among nature silence is not,
on the sandbar, listening to light trot
of ripples of water over still bath
as the flow hit boulders, stones in its path.

The creek's north bank of sand and pebbles stock
a swimming hole off of the pumice rock
bald, majestic and high in sharp contrast
against forest green; we stood there, aghast.

The day was ending; it was getting dark,
overhead the weather had left its mark
of former clouds now isolated from chains,
a sky of blue-greys with marbleized veins.

As we returned, exhausted and content
in the back seat, thinking words to foment,
in complete darkness, scattering each thought,
on paper I wrote in wide letters, wrought.

Charlie and Linda's Condo at the…

Clear Blue Waters

A couple of days at the lake
this early Spring was a grand break,
High-perched without an obstruction
creating a dreamer's fiction,
a calm sailing across the way.
This is a time for fun and play.

A Winter, aged, held on to stay,
for a warm sun we needed to pray.
The weather, often capricious,
did not want a log-fire precious.
The chefs took their turn to show off
with their special menu spin-off.

In a car, chauffeured countryside
through hills high or steep, was the ride;
shorelines, hilltop mansions above.
From cove to cove, to another cove,
we traveled warm with the sun rays
in search of secluded cafés.

Clear blue waters at a distance,
wildflowers nearby with fragrance
that will follow you awhile,
for you are a city exile.
As the day mellowed and then aged
it was time to return, be caged.

The suitcase in trunk of the car,
a last lemonade at the bar;
from everyone, thank you, goodbyes;
we were sad, sad, with sad denies.
We all dreamed, talked of a comeback,
driving on the way back.

Winter

*"With age, my life is decelerating fast.
My body needs a temporary cot to rest
while recounting moments past, and waiting
for the ultimate resting plot."*

One Winter Day Of Snow

*We had a mild Summer
followed by an Autumn,
then an Indian Summer,
sunny, warm and awesome.*

*Snow fell in early morn,
soft, not wanting to hold.
Warm temperatures scorn
a snow that is not bold.*

*There is no heavy coat,
no log, no burning fire,
no boats stopped to float,
no mellow sounds of lyre.*

*The snow is gone, no ice
to skate on and fall;
no hot cider and spice,
no spirited snow brawl.*

*One Winter day of snow
will January know.*

Rebirth

"Dead man's spirit believes in the wisdom of silence!"

Without treatment, survival time after a cardiac arrest is no longer than five minutes. In 2006 Toussaint experienced an arrest following a surgical procedure. I had accompanied him to his hospital room and, fortunately, had not yet left for home when suddenly, in the middle of a sentence, he appeared to fall asleep. Alarmed, I ran out into the hallway to summon help. A Code Blue team quickly assembled and rushed into his room. Meanwhile, because of a fierce thunderstorm earlier that day, the entire hospital was operating solely on auxiliary power.

From the nearby sitting area where I had been escorted, the sound of the paddles and further commotion could be heard. In those moments it seemed that the doctors were continually trying to jumpstart his heart. Again and again the sound radiated. It occurred to me that their efforts were becoming increasingly futile, and the dreaded phone call would soon need to be made to Toussaint's daughters. After ten or so minutes, the sound of the paddles stopped and I braced myself. "Oh, no, it's over," I thought, noticing several attendants heading in my direction. In amazement, I heard: "Well, we have him stabilized." He had survived the arrest.

His daughters, of course, were at his side throughout the week-long ordeal. Suzanne flew in from the East Coast within a matter of hours. Each day, Aimee was at her father's bedside at sunrise.

Another person instrumental during his crisis and recovery was our long-time friend Monica Paulus Ekic, a Registered Nurse. Her caring nature and years of experience helped navigate Toussaint through his recovery. His deep appreciation and respect for this talented woman developed into a warm friendship with Monica and her husband Semir.

Another transition had occurred in Toussaint's life. And, happily for friends and family, it was only temporary.

I Died On July Twenty-One

You must wonder
about my silence,
and not sending some poetry
after my obvious interest
in reading, these past months.

I died on July Twenty-One
in a hospital;
and, thanks to my dear friend
who was at my bedside,
her calls brought in help
and the paddles
to jolt me back to life.

It worked, and here I am,
with pacemaker and defibrillator,
doing rather well,
confined to four walls,
and no car.

Hold Me Up And Stay There

To be confined to a wheelchair
brings often much despair.
We see everything from the same angle;
we get used to it, but it is not ideal.

Stand me up,
hold me up,
I want to stand up.

Standing, I will see how things are to be;
this will make me most happy.
I will feel as part of the crowd,
welcome and even proud.

Hold me up and stay there.
Hold me in an embrace with care,
to feel your body alive against mine,
this will always be divine.

I want to feel your warmth,
hear the rhythm of your breath,
discover your tempting perfume,
and forget the day's gloom.

Hold me up and stay there
while I say my daily prayer
that soon I will return to normal,
you there – when to stand – I am able, once more.

Sunrise, Sunset

So tenuous was his recovery from the cardiac arrest, no one could predict with certainty that Toussaint would be able to travel to Jamaica with Charlie and me five weeks later for the marriage of his daughter Suzanne to Thomas Stofko. A mere three days before the wedding, he was declared well enough to travel. So began a week on the beautiful island, commemorating the many events that had brought us all to this lovely paradise.

It was during the week in Jamaica that his family was reunited for any length of time since the divorce. Fifteen years had eroded enough bitterness to allow both parents to fulfill their daughter's wishes to escort her down the aisle on her wedding day.

You Came With A Smile

So cheerful, you came with a smile,
planning to let time go for quite awhile.
Today, there is no hurry, you told me.
Next three days, this is the way it will be.

Like years past, daughter and father alone,
a live conversation, just like on phone.
With radiant emotions readily seen,
so happy, for it has a long time been.

We shared good news, and all of the other;
often, some things are best if they smother,
to be forgotten, locked in the past,
not even the worst, will forever last.

While writing, I think of you, your young life.
So, a day here and there will be with strife.
Your kindness will wash all of that away;
in your heart, only the best will replay.

So cheerful, I remember your smile.

Daughter Aimee Celine had been married in a lovely wedding several years earlier. The torrential rainstorm on a dreary November day had not seemed to affect the joyous mood inside the beautifully glassed atrium housed in a lovely garden. Toussaint had requested The Poor People of Paris to perform at his daughter's reception.

In spite of all the exuberance, the bitterness over his divorce was still evident in the receiving line: Toussaint opted to position himself on the groom's side of the line, symbolic of his ongoing disassociation from his former wife. Unlike at the Jamaica wedding a few years later, he had not yet been able to put his grievances aside.

This May Be The Time

Your card was nice,
the words warm and kind.
Yes, past two Sundays great
for father and daughter.
This may be the time
to rediscover your father.

I only wanted the best for you,
to guide you the way I knew,
for I never took a course
in being a father.
This may be the time
To rediscover my daughter.

You wanted to be yourself
at a young age
before learning how,
quick to rebel, quick to go.

This may be the time to spend
Sundays together.

Papa Knows Best

As difficult as the marriage had been, he would never regret those years. The marriage had produced his beloved daughters.

His European mannerisms must have at times seemed rigid, even harsh, to his American-born girls. He always had expectations that few parents in the United States would have contemplated. Yet he always adored his daughters in the same way his parents had nurtured him.

These are customs long-ingrained, and only future generations living in modern American society likely could alter them—if indeed anyone decides they need altering.

His devotion is obvious as he describes Suzanne's ever-present sense of responsibility, and Aimee's gift for writing; Suzanne's business acumen, and Aimee's keen mind; the lovely, petite Suzanne, the striking, statuesque Aimee. Through the years, his daughters have been the subjects of many of his poems and letters.

What he instinctively perceives as instructional and nurturing is sometimes viewed by his daughters as stern and disciplinary. It is during such times that both girls baffle him. After all, he declares, he is "their Papa, with sage advice for children – at any age!"

Perhaps the mutual affection shared between father and daughters was never so apparent as when he was emerging from his near-death experience. Whatever the differences between them, the girls were solidly there for him, and he for them.

Under Paris Skies

"A farewell is only for a while.
In time we do get back together,
where no pain and no regrets are."

Toussaint returned to Paris in the Spring of 2008. We were fortunate to accompany him, along with his daughter Suzanne and her husband Tommy. The last time he had visited France was before his daughters were born.

Several highlights of the trip included a return to the Moulin Rouge, where he could almost hear the music that his great-uncle Jose Padilla had performed some seventy-five years before.

He also had the privilege of being invited to read at the Club des poetes, a popular Parisian poetry club in the Left Bank.

That he could share the Paris sights with at least one of his daughters was in itself a very special highlight.

During the second week, Irene Pellicer, his cousin by marriage, invited him to stay at her lovely home in the Paris suburbs. The chic Irene introduced him to various relatives and took him to many Parisian places, including the memorable l' accueil du Maroc restaurant.

His cousin Raymond lived in the same apartment building, and the two discussed the possibility of Toussaint making a return trip to France so that he might renew his relationship with other cousins.

His visit also made possible further collaboration with Arnaud Pellicer, Irene's and Raymond's son, who was composing the music for Toussaint's haunting lyrics, *C'est à toi de quitter.*

On The Soil Of Paris

Once setting foot on the soil of Paris,
we were enthralled by the metropolis;
from across the ocean we left our routine
to live a new dream and sample the cuisine.

I did become a tourist for awhile;
on the spot, became a Francophile
wanting to experience all that is French,
even a covered sky, rain—and the drench.

We took bus tours from the Left Bank,
edging along the Seine river bank
to the Arc de Triomphe, passing palaces,
the Eiffel Tower, sidewalk painters, their canvasses.

From a gliding riverboat in the channels
came a new view of the steeples
piercing the landscape into the skies,
passing nudists basking at sunrise.

This was Paris in the month of May
before the invading crowds arrived for play,
when the cherry trees were not yet blooming,
and the flowers and birds were just awakening.

J'imaginais le Moulin Rouge

Devant l'imposant Moulin et son Rouge
nous sommes en ligne pour rentrer
je discerne tout, les plus simples détails
le publique, les pancartes, les rideaux,
les couleurs vives, rouge, ocre et cuivre.
Je veux retourner au passé
les jours et nuits grandioses
de nos ancêtres aux spectacles, aux concerts.

J'imaginais le Moulin Rouge de ce temps là,
l'enivrement de la musique
l'anticipation de l'entrée sur scène
de belles filles minces, élégantes,
se paradant en costumes menus
les grands éventails couvant
pour aussitôt dévoiler
leurs attributs excitants.

J'imaginais Mistinguett chantant
"Ça c'est Paris" à la musique
de mon grand-oncle
José Padilla Sanchez,
compositeur espagnol,
dans ses années de gloire: vingt-neuf et trente
et de son fameux Paso Doble "Valencia"
et l'inoubliable "El relicario."

J'imaginais Paris, Ville des Lumières,
allègre, éclatante et festive;
les voitures reluisantes
en ligne, leurs chauffeurs en uniformes
leurs occupants en smokings et robe de soirée,
qui lentement déposaient les conviés
sous l'enseigne luminaire
de la porte principale.

Une fois à intérieur, bien placé,
après une coupe de champagne,
un toast à la mémoire de José,
l'orchestre joua des refrains entraînants.
Avec Almarie, ma fille, j'ai dansé une Cha cha
Puis un swing avec Linda
sur la piste touchant l'estrade où Mistinguett
chantait à la musique de mon grand-oncle.

C'était un moment d'émotions
créées par le passée et le présent.
Un rapprochement inoubliable.
Je me sentais en famille proche
avec un lien avec celle d'en temps
J'imaginais mon Grand-Oncle
composant de nouvelles mélodies
pour mes paroles leur donnant de l'entrain.

J'imaginais.

The French Connection

The author is fortunate to have retained ties with his European family. He has remained in close contact with his cousin, Nadia Callejon, a gifted artist in Nimes, France, from his mother's side of the the family. Denise de Guiramand, a prolific writer and researcher residing in Dax, France, from his father's side, has passionately pursued gathering genealogical information on their ancestors.

Toussaint returned to France in less than a year's time. The purpose of this trip was to focus on spending more time with his cousins, many of whom he had not seen on his earlier visit. His Parisian cousin Raymond Pellicer had offered to take him by car throughout France and Spain to accomplish that mission.

After a week in Paris, the two cousins embarked on their adventure. Unfortunately, after touring around for several days, realization set in that they were incompatible travel partners. The trip was rapidly spiraling down from enjoyable to tense to intolerable, and simply was not going to work. So, in a remote region in France, the two parted company.

The determined traveler was not one to pull the plug on his adventure over the mere inconvenience of losing his transportation. Giving up the prospect of seeing his cousins, all of whom were expecting him in various parts of France, was unthinkable. Researching the local train schedule, Toussaint continued his journey by rail. He was able to communicate the change of plans to his relatives and, at every destination, a cousin was on hand to welcome him at the station.

After spending a few enjoyable days with cousins Jean-Claude and Nicole Pellicer at his art studio in Montpelier, he trained to Cannes, home of his cousin Rosemarie Avrillon. The elegance of the place made him feel as though he had arrived in Hollywood. He and his glamorous cousin saw the sights of her city, and visited Nice and Monaco as well.

Continuing his travels by rail, he crossed over into Spain for several days. There, he was the guest of prolific Catalan writer Victor Peris i Brau and his family in the toney Valencia region of Tavernes de Valdignia.

Upon his return to Paris, he was an overnight guest of poet and scientist Laurent Seugnet, a former Washington University affiliate. Seugnet took

Toussaint to the eclectic Chat Noir Café and Club in the lively Belleville District for a profound literary interpretation delivered by a Parisian actor. The Chat Noir is an established part of the Parisian theatre scene.

Toussaint spent his remaining time in Paris with his stylish cousin Irene who once again graciously welcomed him into her home. There, he had the opportunity to visit various members of Irene's family, including another cousin, Janine Pellicer.

The author had realized his dream of re-connecting with his European cousins and had experienced the joy of returning to his beloved Spain, and Valencia.

The Sun Of Spain

How I would like to feel again the sun of Spain,
the warmth of the rays bathing the grapes' domain;
the hot air by noon announcing time for a siesta,
vineyards, olive trees, a snowless mountain vista.

In the distance, the heat forming a mirage
of blurred fields, shadowed groves in a montage,
recalling the past, affirming the day, depicting the future
as a repeat of the landscape under the same azure.

How I would like to feel again the sun of Spain,
let my skin bronze a little each day, not expecting rain;
then wait for the cool evening to venture out,
dance hard on the cobblestones until worn out.

Let my spirits fly at the sounds of "Valencia,"
thanking my great uncle for this musical fantasia
with sounds of the rushing of the bull in a Paso Doble,
cape flairs, the matador's pivots, the crowds shouting, "Ole!"

How I would like to feel again the sun of Spain
until the cool breeze of the sea sings its refrain.

Epilogue

Being in the winter of one's life does not necessarily mean that one ceases to enjoy.

For Toussaint, there are concerts to attend, cabarets to enjoy, poems to write and recite at various events, contests to win, quality times to arrange with his daughters, photographs to take, movies to see, visits to schedule at the VA and the gym, road trips to plan, old friendships to nurture, and new ones to discover.

To accommodate all that, perhaps Winter needs to be the longest season in one's lifetime. There certainly never seems to be sufficient time in the earlier seasons to accomplish what most consider a full life.

These concluding poems, written through the years, are selections from Marcel Toussaint's vast repertoire. They seem to capture a sampling of the breadth of the poet's subjects. Perhaps some are a direct result of his life experiences. Others may reside solely within his imaginative mind.

Only the author knows for certain.

It Is For You To Leave

(C'est à toi de quitter)

We lived together, much too long.
Yes, our love lost its springtime;
yes, we are both exhausted
from faded words of a love gone.

You are still here; you don't seem to leave.
To see you every day, I can no more suffer.
Of a deep silence, we are both taken.
Your daily presence holds up my life.

It is for you to leave
from a love gone.

You persist to remain at my side.
You know it; it is final, you must leave.
The indefinite tomorrow has a need for space
from a finished romance with no room to spare.

It is for you to leave
from a love gone.

Don't imagine there may be some hope.
To be together is no more a duty,
emotions, passion now extinct,
their vigor gone without an embrace.

We lived together, much too long.
Yes, our love lost its springtime;
yes, we are both exhausted
from faded words of a love gone.

It is for you to leave
from a love gone.
From a love gone
it is for you to leave.

Her Amorous Body

Uncovered breasts honey-gold baked
in the sun, delicate slippery skin with oils,
a light wildflower fragrance from the islands,
two blushing nipples seek the blue sky.

Her emotions, young, explore.

Under dark glasses her eyes are open,
her legs stretched on the sand.
The water advances, retires, wets her feet; still.
she follows the hypnotic flight of birds from the sea.

A blossom of love in her dreams.

Desire held back, ready to explode
makes her amorous body vibrate whole.
She dreams of a laissez-aller for two,
passionate young bodies interlaced.

Her amorous body, vibrant, plays.

At the base of her breast, a gentle hand enjoys
pushing high toward the end, emotions of youth.
She arches her body, repeating with force,
her hips rebound and fall. She moans.

Exhausted, her body satisfied.

Who In The World Are You?

I look at you with no feelings.
You are here every day, so what?
How is it that you are?
Who in the world are you?

I have lost the reason.
Is it possible that we have
agreed to share the rent,
the coolness of the air,
the kitchen with a faucet that leaks,
the bathroom that was meant just for one?
Who in the world are you?

How is it that we share a bedroom,
that you change your clothes without care
while I am just there?
Your reflection fills the mirror on the door;
as I glance coldly, I find no pleasure,
no hope, no interest, no future.
Who in the world are you?

As if by myself,
naked, I lie on the bed,
cold, a vision blurred
by a profound emptiness;
and there you are the same!
Who in the world are you?

How is it that you are there?
You, yourself! Me, myself!
Why is it that you are there?
A blank shell, with no name;
a face with no color, with no words.
Any would be the same, unheard.
Who in the world are you?

I have lost the reason.
Is it possible that we have
agreed to share the rent,
the coolness of the air,
the kitchen with a faucet that leaks,
the bathroom that was meant just for one?
Who in the world are you?

Overused and abused, why should I utter
a meaningless word. Love?
Who in the world are you? Love?
Who in the world are you? Love?
Who in the hell, are you?

Eternal Life

To feel young lasts
past the superficial,
the physical pillages of times.
For it is an emotional state
lodged in our heart, deep inside us.

No mirror will reflect it.
No mirror will distort it.
No mirror will lie about its youthfulness,
about its joyfulness,
about the springtime there forever.

To anticipate that we will return allows for hope,
but we may not leave.
We can live on forever
by contributing our time,
with kindness for others,
with comforting words to those in need,
by writing meaningful thoughts,
by creating works of art,
by alleviating the misery of the suffering.

Great contributors have dignified our civilization;
they have never died.
Their words, their music, their thoughts,
their deeds are present today,
each year, more important to all of us.

We must see if we have something to contribute,
as this will give us eternal life
in the minds of following generations.
Our spirit lingers into the memories of others,
and seldom vanishes in time.

She Drives A Red Convertible

She drives a red convertible,
declares she gets anywhere,
faster than anyone else,
for it is a Mercedes Sports.

She often is stopped,
speeding on the highway,
pulled over from the road,
a young traffic officer coming to her side.

She receives him with a smile
with that innocent look.
"I should not have done that!
I was naughty! You will excuse me?"

The officers always compliment her
on her excellent choice of car.
She delights in thanking them each time
as she performs her pampered housewife act.

"Officer, this car gets away from me;
it is hard to judge the speed!"
She opens slowly her purse
for license, insurance papers.

She fumbles, finding nothing,
rearranging her diamond on her finger,
making sure to make it sparkle
in the sunlight, the roof pulled down.

She plays the rich wife part,
cajoled by money and jewels
à la Zsa Zsa Gabor, Hollywood style,
her blond hair flying in the breeze.

But her approach does not always work.
She collects tickets by the dozen,
has them fixed by a lawyer
who sees in her a return customer.

Living Without

Years have passed living without,
without the things I grew up with,
memories of the past,
my parents,
my life growing up
overseas.

When young,
with friends, quite happy.
Oh, why did I marry?

Years have passed living without,
without windows in basements,
apartment efficiency,
squeezed,
my spirits in disarray.
You, living high,
in my house.

When young,
with friends, quite happy.
Oh, why did I marry?

Now, free of you, without,
without driving me to despair,
without your rotten temperament,
without your nasty insults,
without your endless belligerence,
I am.

When young,
with friends, quite happy.
Oh, why did I marry?

Observing From The Corner

In the neighborhood café,
the light was dim,
hardly reaching the corner.
She liked corners.
Almost unnoticed,
she observed the clientele.

As a writer, she wrote all there is to tell
about the aging older crowd:
mannerisms,
"costumes of the past,"
worn day in, day out,
fading along with their lives,
threads hanging, seams coming apart.

She took notes on their walking,
slowing down to soon stop.
With words, she painted their faces shrunk,
skin crinkled, teeth gone,
their hands shaking, often spilling coffee
too hot, too strong for them to handle.

They had names she had chosen herself.
She cared.
She would know
who had been missing for a while.
Silently she would whisper the names
and a prayer.
For they were on their way
to Heaven.

Reflective Reflection

Looking into the silvery surface of the mirror
is like looking into the reflecting ripples
of clear, mostly tranquil waters.

On the mirror, the ripples are immovable,
wrinkles engraved on the surface of the face
from emotions, smiles, anger, sorrows and laughter.

Nothing in this enduring stillness,
on this silvery surface of the mirror,
will distort the ripples of time.

Truth is there, cold, precise, reflected,
while you become reflective of your etched past
chiseled into the grooves of your advancing age.

Young Again

Flopped on the lounge chair
on the front porch,
I look at a darkening sky.
The day has aged,
an orange sun retiring,
clouds of copper turning grey.

The invading darkness will hide
the wrinkles of my face;
stars do not care,
the moon will not shine enough
to give my age away.
I feel young again.

Pale Face

A face pale
erased into the night,
leaning on the window.
The outside light glows
an ivory white,
elegant, sculptured,
a bust in a museum.
No smile, no warmth, still,
marble of years past.
This pale face will last.

Memories Are Forever

Memories are forever.
They keep your heart warm
with a love unending,
passing only to be rejoined.

A love remains constant,
remembering the fun times,
the close moments spent by the bonfires
with friends in the autumn woods,
the fun stories shared by the fireplace
inside, when the winters got too bold.

A love exploring cities, countries, the world,
returns home for a rest and new plans for more.
This love does not want us to be sad as it travels.
It wants us to keep on echoing the past,
staying forever close in shared memories,
for there is happiness in having been together.
Memories are forever.

To Be Remembered

To be remembered,
I hope,
able to write
possibly with some style,
at times clever, often sad,
happy with spring and the like.

To be remembered,
I hope,
as a writer
good or bad,
myself, no one else,
to be or not to be a Shakespeare,
strive I do not.

To label myself a poet,
should I, should I not?
A writer who writes poetry?
Let the readers decide
in time.
Am I, am I not?
To be remembered,
I hope.

My words uttered
at least once
will continue their journey,
echoed into space,
forever.
To be remembered.

The Sole Authority

After a long life we pretend to be wise,
something that cannot be measured.
We find ourselves the sole authority
in many subjects on the skills of life,
a connoisseur of love and heartbreaks.
We tell everyone what is wrong with them.

After a long life we think we have it all,
the answers to everything.
We interrupt conversations to add our own
two-cents worth to stand above the others.
We are so much better than they are!
We seem pleased to make them feel inadequate.

After a long life we think we were the best of parents;
we correct children who are not our own,
raise our eyebrows on the loose mores of the day,
state, "This generation is going to hell!"
while we will sit on a white cloud in heaven
that we're not sure will hold us up forever.

After a long life we think we must control
the scientific advances that scare us,
saying that in the good old days
we lived happily without them;
that we are tampering with nature,
and will bring on the inevitable doomsday.

After a long life we would do well
to contemplate the past, the present,
and venture into our short-timed future,
leaving others free to stumble and recover,
to discover how to make our old days
healthy without pain, without policing them.

The Butterfly

You are so ethereal and so fragile.
You conserve energy so dutiful
to stay delicate, fresh and beautiful,
a butterfly with a great profile.

Graceful, you handle yourself very light,
your wings brilliant, like colorful flowers,
quickly hiding at first sign of showers,
paper-thin stained glass in flickering flight.

After long day you must stop at sundown
with the disappearing sun's golden rays
shining low, signaling time-up for plays.
For butterflies flying, comes a rest down.

The day is for your glory, not the night,
for the fields with flowers you need to view.
I shall wait for daybreak after the dew,
a warming sun and your spirited flight.

In Rancor Or To Adore

The sun has set
and the day closed its net.
Yesterday is memory, nothing more,
lost to rancor or alive for in the future to adore.

Photo Album

Saint Pellicer with family posing on army vehicle at the family farm on the beach in Morocco.

(Right) Saint Pellicer's Great Uncle, Spanish composer, Jose Padilla.

(Far Right) Saint Pellicer's sister, Josephine, as a Spanish señorita.

(Above) Saint Pellicer "Les Yeux."

(Right) Saint Pellicer at the entry gate of the family home in Rabat.

(Far Right) On the beach in Morocco holding his young cousin, Martine.

Saint Pellicer as a young man and in uniform.

(Above) The author performing in a skit at the Army base in Boeblingen, Germany.

(Above) The author's sister, Josephine, with her daughter, Odette.

(Right) Saint Pellicer with his mother on the family farm, seaside in Morocco.

(Above) The author's first photograph on U.S. soil: at the home of his sponsors, Mr. and Mrs. Joseph Comer.

(Below) The family's vineyard in Spain.

(Above) Saint Pellicer in 1955 convertible in Forest Park, Saint Louis, Missouri.

(Above) Saint Pellicer with his sister, Odette, as his dance partner.

(Above) Emil Saint Pellicer conducts a dance class.

(Right and Below) A proper curtsey, under the watchful eye of Instructor Saint Pellicer at the home of Madame Lemoine Skinner.

Vouziers, a castle on the Missouri River bluffs, home of society matron Anne Desloge Werner.

(Right) Saint Pellicer around age 30.

(Below) 1961 "Promenade Along the Bridges of Paris" a Famous-Barr International event.

(Above) Saint Pellicer receives students arriving for lessons at his Conservatoire on Clayton Road.

(Below) The fabled Nash Ambassador.

St. Pellicer
6317 Clayton Rd
Clayton
ATHLETIC DUELING

(Above) Duelers at the Saint Pellicer Conservatoire on Clayton Road.

(Right) Maitre d' Armes Saint Pellicer at TV studio with Regis Philbin.

(Below) Saint Pellicer instructs student, Susan Feldman, in use of cane for self defense.

(Below) Master of Arms Stanley Saint Pellicer at the Conservatoire.

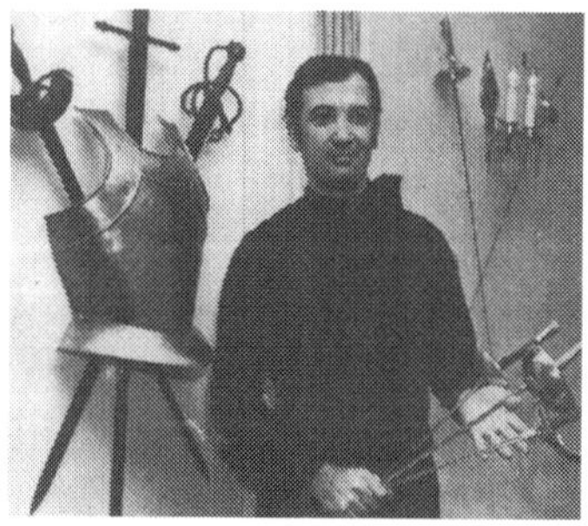

(Left) Carol Sitzwohl and opponent, with author (in background). Saint Pellicer invented the modern version of "Athletic Dueling," where matches are fought "in the round."

(Far Left) Suzanne Almarie with baby sister, Aimee Celine.

(Left) Suzanne as a little girl.

(Below) Aimee Celine with Talbot, the family Poodle (French, of course!).

Papa's Girls

(Above) Suzanne at Christmas time.

(Right) Suzanne on Prom night. (Note painting of Saint Pellicer's mother in background.)

(Left) Saint Pellicer, the College Administrator.

(Left) Christine Peick, songstress and founder of Bluegrass band, Raven Moon.

(Below) The author with Christine Peick.

(Left) Farshid Soltanshahi, guitarist and leader of Latin/ Gypsy musical ensemble, Farshid Etniko.

(Right) Violin virtuoso Christopher Voelker performs at New Year's Eve party at the Dahlheimers, 2003.

(Left) Toussaint at 1997 CD release party with Poor People of Paris chanteuse, Elsie Parker and Keyboard artist, Donita Bauer.

(Right) Bassist, Wayne Coniglio and Elsie Parker, chanteuse and instrumentalist with The Poor People of Paris.

(Below) Elsie performs at Brandts with keyboard artist, Michael Carosello.

(Left) Rusty Werner, (stage name Rusty LaDon) sings at Dahlheimers' New Year's Eve Soiree.

(Right) Keyboard artist and singer, Curt Landes.

(Right) Charlie and Linda Dahlheimer at a concert by The Poor People of Paris at the Carriage House in Soulard.

(Left) Bill Ballard and Kathy Atwood at a New Year's Eve Soiree in Benton Park.

(Left) The author surrounded with beauty: from left: His daughter, Aimee Celine, Christine Peick, Toussaint, Linda Dahlheimer, Sylvie Esparel and Elsie Parker.

(Above) Owl Creek Farm.

(Left) Owl Creek Farm Esquire, Bill Ballard, tends the grill.

(Left) Marcel Toussaint, Linda Dahlheimer, Brett Cervantes and Charlie Dahlheimer at Mihalis Lounge.

(Below) Charlie Dahlheimer, Alan and Pam Appt, and Linda Dahlheimer at the Carriage House in Soulard.

(Left) Toussaint reads poetry at Cafe de France.

(Below) Linda Dahlheimer and Marcel Toussaint at Cafe de France.

(Above) Linda with bandleader, composer and arranger, Stan Fornaszewski at Erato Wine Bar. Fornaszewski is setting Toussaint's "Saint Lou-ie, Saint Lou-ie" to music.

(Above) Saint Pellicer at a Moroccan restaurant in the Paris suburbs.
(Top, Right) with daughter Suzanne Almarie in Luxembourg Gardens, Paris.
(Inset) The author with cousin Irene, her son Arnaud (left) and cousin Nicole.

(Right) The author's cousin, Arnaud, a composer with whom Marcel has been collaborating.

The author's daughter, Suzanne Almarie, with husband, Tommy, outside the Moulin Rouge.

Toussaint with cousin, Irene Pellicer, in Paris.

(Right) At the Moulin Rouge in May, 2008: Tom and Suzanne Stofko, Charlie and Linda Dahlheimer and Marcel Toussaint.

(Left and Below) While in Paris, Marcel Toussaint was invited to read his poetry at the Club des poetes.

(Right) The author with Club des poetes owner, Blaise Rosnay.

(Left) Three-time Gold Medalist Marcel Toussaint with Pete McBrady, assistant director of Veteran's Administration in Saint Louis, at 2009 awards ceremony .

The Jamaica Wedding

(Above) The bride, Marcel's daughter, Suzanne Almarie (center) with groom Tom Stofko (right); Marcel's daughter Aimee Celine (left) with the groom's nieces as flower bearers.

(Above) Marcel taking a break amid the Jamaican Palms.

(Above) Marcel Toussaint with daughter Aimee Celine in Ocho Rios.

(Right) The Bride and Groom just after the ceremony in church overlooking the sea.

(Above) Au bord de l'eau, daughter Suzanne Almarie's cottage on Maryland's Eastern Shores, served as the author's summer retreat for many years.

(Above) Suzanne on the pier at Au bord de l'eau.

(Left) Toussaint draws poetic inspiration from the relaxing waters at Au bord de l'eau.

(Right) Always the Maitre d' Armes, Toussaint in a mock duel with waiter at seaside restaurant in Rehoboth Beach, Delaware.

(Left) The narrator gains insight into Toussaint's multi-faceted career while visiting at the Eastern Shores. Victoria returns from a stroll.

Index of Press Coverage

1957 *The SACom Scene*, Article regarding Saint Pellicer's contest in Stuttgart
1959 *france-amerique*, Saint Pellicer first place winner in Bastille Day event.
1960 *Kirkwood Cotillion*, Announces new classes directed by Saint Pellicer
1960 *Junior League*, Announcing new season of Saturday Morning Dance Classes
1960 *The Council Ring*, Saint Pellicer guest speaker on Morocco at Cahokia High School
1960 *Globe-Democrat*, Photos and story about dancing teacher Saint Pellicer
1960 *Greenbriar Country Club News*, Article about Saint Pellicer's teaching technique
1960 *Greenbriar Country Club News*, Another story on Saint Pellicer's teaching style
1960 *Holiday* magazine, Saint Pellicer photographed with students at Union Ballroom
1960 *Ballroom Dance Magazine*, Story on Saint Pellicer's dancing and deportment classes
1961 *Kirkwood Cotillion*, Saint Pellicer directs numerous events at Westborough Country Club
1961 *Junior League*, Announces new season of Saturday Morning Dance Classes
1961 *Globe-Democrat*, Saint Pellicer directs *Fleur-de-lis Ball* in Chase Park Plaza Khorassan Room
1961 *Kirkwood Cotillion*, Announces new dance classes for Saint Pellicer
1961 *Alliance Française*, Saint Pellicer co-hosts French Conversation Tea on Chase Park Plaza Roof
1961 *Globe-Democrat*, Saint Pellicer directed *Promenade to Bridges in Paris* at *International. Living* event
1961 *Globe-Democrat*, Saint Pellicer directed *Colorful Mexico*, *International Living*, danced the *Paso Doble*
1961 *france-amerique*, *International. Living* event at Famous-Barr Clayton Store
1961 *france-amerique*, *International Living* event at Famous-Barr, related story
1962 *Post-Dispatch*, Saint Pellicer listed among eighty-two donors in Saint Louis Symphony article
1962 *Globe-Democrat*, Saint Pellicer danced French Minuet at dinner dance
1962 *Globe-Democrat*, Saint Pellicer in reception honoring French on Chase Park Plaza Roof
1962 *Post-Dispatch*, Saint Pellicer interviewed for lead story on "*How Children Learn Manners*"
1962 *france-amerique*, Story about Saint Pellicer's dancing salon at Union Ballroom
1963 *Globe-Democrat*, Fulbright Scholar special guest at Union Ballroom for Alliance Française
1963 *Globe-Democrat*, Saint Pellicer practicing for *Dancing Now and Then* event at Union Ballroom
1963 *Missouri Historical*, Story on *Dancing-Now and Then*, Chase Park Plaza Khorassan Room
1963 *Post-Dispatch*, Saint Pellicer's directs *Dancing-Now and Then*, Chase Park Plaza Khorassan Room
1963 *Dance Programme*, Saint Pellicer directs event for Anne Desloge at Vouziers
1963 *Post-Dispatch*, Dance awards given at Union Ballroom recital
1963 *Globe Democrat*, Dance awards given at Union Ballroom recital
1963 *County Obsever*, Saint Pellicer to go to New York for fencing classes
1963 *Globe-Democrat*, Saturday Morning Classes to start at Union Ballroom
1963 *Post-Dispatch*, Learning the "Pachanga" at Union Ballroom
1963 *Alliance Française*, Story about Saint Pellicer's dancing studio
1963 *Alliance Française*, Grand Ballet Classique visits Saint Pellicer's Union Ballroom
1964 *Post-Dispatch*, Maurice Bruziere special guest at Union Ballroom for Alliance Française
1964 *Globe-Democrat*, Alliance Française meet at Union Ballroom
1964 *Globe-Democrat*, Saint Pellicer holds Parents Day at Union Ballroom for Saturday Morning Class
1964 *Post-Dispatch*, Saint Pellicer acknowledged at Mayor's Tree Proclamation Ceremony
1964 *Globe-Democrat*, Saint Pellicer announces formal opening of Conservatoire
1964 *Post-Dispatch*, Saint Pellicer announces formal opening of Conservatoire
1964 *Globe-Democrat*, Story on Saint Pellicer's all-day dance contest at Conservatoire
1965 *Globe-Democrat*, Saint Pellicer to be featured on Charlotte Peters Show again
1965 *Ballroom Dance Magazine*, Story on Saint Pellicer's new dance, "The Pelican"
1965 *Globe-Democrat*, Saint Pellicer participates in Grand International Ball, Khorassan Room

1965 *Post-Dispatch*, Saint Pellicer's Awards Presentation at Conservatoire
1965 *Le Cercle d'Escrime*, Fencing article about Saint Pellicer
1965 *Globe-Democrat*, Saint Pellicer co-directs Summer Classes at Park Plaza with Alliance Française
1965 *Le Cercle d/Escrime,* Story on Saint Pellicer;s youth in Morocco
1965 *Post-Dispatch*, Saint Pellicer co-directs Summer Classes at Park Plaza with Alliance Française
1965 *Post-Dispatch*, Saint Pellicer's involvement in *International Ball* at Chase Park Plaza
1965 *Forest Hills*, Saint Pellicer directed a Hootenanny at Forest Hills Country Club
1965 *Globe-Democrat*, European students visit Saint Pellicer's Conservatoire
1965 *Post-Dispatch*, Saint Pellicer coordinated Turkish Fencing Demo at Washington University
1965 *The Gospel Voice*, Saint Pellicer's involvement in the Panorama '65 Fair
1965 *Baden News/Press*, Saint Pellicer arranged a program for a Boy Scouts Fencing Demo
1966 *Metro-East Journal*, "Outdoor Fencing," story on Saint Pellicer
1967 *St. Louis University Magazine*, "En Garde," story on Saint Pellicer by Pat Cronin
1967 *Globe-Democrat*, Saint Pellicer quoted on lecture at Saint Louis University
1967 *Metro-East Journal*, Three-page coverage on Saint Pellicer at Conservatoire
1968 *Post-Dispatch*, A story about Saint Pellicer entitled "Dueling for Sport."
1968 *Granite City Press Record*, "Saint Pellicer Lectures at Southern Illinois University"
1968 *The Alton Telegraph*, "Saint Pellicer Lecture at Southern Illinois University"
1968 *Post-Dispatch Sunday Pictures*, three pages on Dueling at Saint Pellicer's Conservatoire
1969 *St. Louis County Observer*, "Fencing Both Sport, Therapy," story on Saint Pellicer
1969 *Mercantile News*, "Fencing Recommended for Everyone," article on Saint Pellicer
1969 *Metro-East Journal*, "Weekend d'Artagnan." Full-page story about Saint Pellicer
1970 *Tolle Lege*, "St. Augustinian Academy. Touche," story on Saint Pellicer
1970 *Post-Dispatch*, "Auxiliary Costume Ball. Duel," story about Saint Pellicer
1970 *Globe-Democrat*, "Isabella of Spain Tournament, Spanish International Pavillion"
1970 *Replay Amateur Sports*, "Replay Sponsors a tournament," involving Saint Pellicer
1970 *Junior College News*, "Saint Pellicer Lectures at Forest Park Community College"
1970 *Globe-Democrat*, "Mai Fete, 17th Century Duel," story on Saint Pellicer
1970 *Post-Dispatch*, "17th Century Duel, Mai Fete," story pertaining to Saint Pellicer
1972 *Athletic Dueling News*, Saint Pellicer featured in "Athletic Dueling Tourney Winners"
1972 *Community News*, "Saint Pellicer Conducts Dueling Seminar"
1973 *Community News*, Saint Pellicer featured in "Athletic Dueling Tournois Winners
1973 *Post-Dispatch*, Saint Pellicer featured in "Dueling Awards Given"
1973 *St. Louis County Star-Clayton Citizen*, "Dueling for Executives," story on Saint Pellicer
1973 *Community News*, Saint Pellicer gives "Course in Fencing, Dueling Offered at Junior College"
1973 *TV Guide, TV Facts* Salutes Saint Pellicer
1973 *Globe-Democrat*, Saint Pellicer Made 34th television appearance on Regis Philbin
1973 *Rutgers Observer Faulkner,* Student of Saint Pellicer accepts reward
1974 *Apartment Living*, Story on Saint Pellicer's school programs.
1974 *Post-Dispatch*, Saint Pellicer featured in "New Dueling Sport Taught at UMSL, FVCC"
1974 *UMSL Current*, "Dueling: A Refreshing Alternative," story about Saint Pellicer
1975 *St. Louis Globe Democrat,* Saint Pellicer's programs in high schools and colleges
1975 *University News,* Article on Saint Pellicer's classes at Saint Louis University
1975 *St. Louis Globe Democrat* Story on Saint Pellicer and Carondelet Foundry
1975 *Post-Dispatch*, Story on Saint Pellicer and John Cullin, Chairman at Carondelet Foundry
1975 *Globe-Democrat*, "Home is Where the Business Is," story on Saint Pellicer

Accueil du Maroc, l', 198
Adams Mark Hotel, 168
Algonquin Country Club, 82
Alliance Francaise, 85-87, 95
Alton Telegraph, 91
America At The Millennium, 175
American Athletic Dueling Ass'n, 92, 97
Annunciata Church, 82
Apartment Living, 93, 107
Appt, Alan and Pam, 165, 169, 178, 231
Athletic Dueling News, 91
Atlanta, Georgia, 68, 70
Atlas Contractors, 57
Atwood, Kathy, 169, 230
Au bord de l'eau, 144-147, 235
Avrillon, Rosemarie, 202
Baker, Josephine, 37
Ballard, Bill, 150-151, 163, 169, 184-185, 230
Ballroom Dance Magazine, 83, 86
Balmar Farm, 150-151
Bates, Mrs. Charles, II, 83
Bauer, Donita, 157
Bellerive Country Club, 82
Belleville High 12 Club, 94
Belz, Aaron, 178
Benoist, Mrs. Howard, Jr., 83
Benton Park, 162-165, 168
Boeblingen, Germany, 74, 87, 225
Brandt's Café, 157, 168, 229
Broeke, Alois, 37
Bruziere, Maurice, 85
Burroughs, John, High School, 94
Café de France, 168, 231
Café Eau, 168
Nadia Callejon, 202
Cannes, 202
Carney, Jack, 95
Carondelet Foundry, 96-97
Carosello, Michael, 229
Carter, Derek and Josephine, 35, 76, 224, 225
Casablanca, Morocco, 44, 54, 121
Casey, Jan and Bob, 169
Cervantes, Alfonso J., 97
Cervantes, Brett, 169
Charles, Ray, 157
Chase Park Plaza, 83, 85-87, 95
Chat Noir Café, 202-203
Cheshire Inn, 86
Chevalier, Maurice, 37, 85
Childers, Gerry and Jean, 169
Clayton High School, 94
Club de Poetes, 198, 233
Coleman Orchestra, The Bob, 157
College des Oranges, 41
Comer, Joseph, 58
Comer, Odette and William, 54, 58, 69, 81, 86, 226
Community News, 92
Coniglio, Wayne, 157, 165, 168, 229
Conservatoire de Musique, 41, 53
Conservatoire de Rabat, 87
Conte, Dr., 54, 55
County Observer, 91
Crossing, The, 168
Culling, John H., 96-97
Dahlheimer, Charles and Linda, 39, 157, 162-169, 178, 187, 190, 198, 228, 230, 231, 233
Dahlheimer, Michael, 165
Dancing Now and Then, 85
Davis, Kecia, 168
Dax, France, 202
De Andreas High School, 94
De Guiramand, Denise, 202
De Havilland, Olivia, 75
De Moret, Madame Anne Marie, 81
Desloge, Anne, 88
Desloge, Mrs. Bernard F., 83
Dodds, Mrs. James, 95
Ehrenreich, Mrs. Bernard, 95
Ekic, Semir and Monica, 190
Embassy Ballroom, 84, 85-86
Erato Wine Bar, 231
Erden, Yucel, 91
Esparel, Sylvie, 169, 230
Famous Barr Company, 83, 227
Farshid Etniko, 168, 228
Faulkner, Michael, 92
Feldman, Susan, 226
Fender, Harry, 97
Ferguson High School, 94
Finale, 168
Fleur de Lis Dances, 82
Fleur de Lis Debutante Ball, 83
Florissant Valley Junior College, 94
Focal Point, The, 155, 168
Forest Park Community College, 91, 94
Fornaszewski, Stan, 168, 231
Fort Carson, Colorado, 63
Fort Lee, Virginia, 65
Fort Leonard Wood, Missouri, 61
Fort McPherson, Georgia, 66, 68
Fox, Dr. Michael, 94
France Amerique, 84
French Conversation Tea, 85

Gaslight Square, 87, 164
Goddard, Bob, 92
Goertz, Marc, 85
Grand Ballet Classique, 85
Grand International Ball, 86
Granite City Press Record, 91
Gravenhorst, Ted and Edna, 169
Greenbriar Country Club, 82
Hall, Leonard, 184
Harris Teachers College, 87
Holiday magazine, 83
Humane Society, 135
International Living Event, 83
JaBoni, 169
Jamaica, 195, 234
Junior League, 84
Kann, Stan, 168
Kaufman, Odette and Rick, 178, 225
KDNL-30, 95
Kenitra, Morocco, 58
Kern, Jerome, 37
KFUO Radio, 87, 95
Khorassan Room, 83, 85-86
Kirkwood Cotillion, 82
KMOX Radio, 95
KMOX-CBS, 95
Knight, Mrs. Newell, 85
Koplar, Mrs. Harold, 95
KRCH Radio, 95
Kreisman, Jim, 164
KSD Radio, 95
KSD-NBC, 95
KSHE Radio, 95
KTVI-11, 95
KXOK Radio, 95
Landes, Curt, 168, 229
Le Chateau, 100
Le Grand, Michel, 165
Lindbergh High School, 94
Loretto Hilton Theater, 151
Luepker, Martie and Sue, 168, 173
Lutheran High South, 94
Lynn, Gene, 168
Madrid, 37
Madrid Conservatory, 37
Mahannah, Jan, 164
Mahler, Jacob, 81-84
Maisonette Francaise, 85-86
Maitre D'Armes, 91
Marambaud, Madame, 57
Mary Institute, 84
Maryland Plaza Redevelopment Corp., 97
McBrady, Pete, 233
Mercantile News, 91
Metro East Journal, 91
Meyer, Mrs. Donald J., 83
Meyers, Dianne, 168
Mihalis, 168, 231
Missouri Botannical Gardens, 168
Missouri Historical Society, 85
Mistinguett, 37-38
Modern Arts Museum, 178
Monaco, 202
Montaldo's, 87, 89
Montpellier, 202
Moulin Rouge, 35, 37-39, 198, 200-201, 232, 233
Mower, Mrs. Edward J., Jr., 83
Mullins, Mrs. Fristoe Mullins, 83
Munich, Germany, 75
Muny at Forest Park, 168
Murray, Arthur, 81
National Public Radio, 175
National Veterans Poetry Anthology, 179
New York City, 91
Nice, France, 202
Nimes, France, 202
Notre Dame High School, 94
Notre Dame University, 91
Obama, Barak, 179
Old Warson Country Club, 82
Orthwein, Linda Rand, 84
Owl Creek Farm, 184-185, 230
Padilla, Jose, 37, 38, 198
Padilla, Sanchez Maria Gracia, 16, 18, 23, 44, 48, 57, 69, 95, 101, 225
Panorama '65 Fair, 87
Panzer Kaserne, Germany, 74, 87
Paris, France, 35, 37, 39, 198-199, 202, 232-233
Parker, Elsie, 157, 163, 165-166, 169, 228-229
Parks College, 35
Paulus, Monica , 190
Peick, Bill, 155, 174
Peick, Christine, 154-155, 163, 168, 174, 178, 228
Pelican, The, 86
Pellicer, Arnaud, 198, 232
Pellicer, Irene, 198, 202, 232
Pellicer, Janine, 202
Pellicer, Jean-Claude, 202
Pellicer, Nicole, 202, 232
Pellicer, Raymond, 202
Peris i Brau, Victor, 202
Peters, Charlotte, 95
Philbin, Regis, 92, 95, 226
Piaff, Edith, 165

Pony Espresso, 155
Poor People of Paris, The, 157, 163, 165-168, 182, 196, 229
Port Lyautey, Morocco, 58
Possum Trot Farm, 184
Powell Hall, 157, 163
Powers, Mrs. Pierce, 86
Presley, Elvis, 75
Previn, Andre, 85
Pulitzer, Mrs. Joseph, Jr., 83
Rabat, Morocco, 16, 17, 32, 35, 41, 57
Radio-Maroc, 41, 53
Raven Moon, 155, 168, 228
Reichard, Ron, 165
Ritter, Cardinal Joseph E., 83
Ritz Carlton, 168
Rosnay, Blaise, 233
Rutgers Observer, 92
Rutgers University, 92
Rutledge, Mrs. Thomas G., 83
Saint Louis Art Museum, 168
Saint Louis Council on World Affairs, 86, 87
Saint Louis Country Club, 82
St. Louis County Star, 92
St. Louis Globe Democrat, 53, 57, 68, 75, 82-87, 91, 93, 97, 107
St. Louis Post Dispatch, 84-86, 91-92, 97, 102
Saint Louis Symphony Orchestra, 85
Saint Louis University, 35, 91, 93, 96, 97
St. Louis Writers Guild, 175, 178
Saint Pellicer Conservatoire, 86-87, 91-95, 102, 227
Saint Pellicer, Aimee Celine, 104, 107, 124-127, 196-197, 228, 234
Saint Pellicer, Raymond Bonancia, 16, 18, 21, 44, 57, 69, 95, 107, 112-113
Saint Pellicer, Suzanne Almarie, 39, 103, 107, 124-127, 135, 144, 195, 197-198, 232-234
Salle d' Armes, 102, 108
Santelli, Georgio, 91
Saturday Morning Dance Class, 83-87
Schlafly, Mrs. Robert F., 83
Schlafly Tap Room, 168
Seugnet, Laurent, 202
Shyrock Auditorium, 167
Sidi Slimane, Morocco, 57
Sitzwohl, Carol, 226
SIU Carbondale, 166
SIU Edwardsville, 91, 94
Skinner, Mrs. Lemoine, Jr., 81, 83-84
Smiley, Jack, 169
Soltanshahi, Farshid, 168, 228
Southern Illinois Symphony, 167
Spanish Pavillion, 91
Stofko, Thomas, 195, 198, 232-234
Stuttgart, Germany, 74
Sullivan, Ed, 74-75
Swing Set, 168
Temple Israel, 84
Trenet, Charles, 165
Truffles, 168
Turkish Olympic Fencing Team, 91
TV Guide, 92
U.S. Air Force, 57
U.S. Army, 61, 75-77, 87
UMSL, 93
Valencia, Spain, 202-203
Valli, Marise, 41
Veterans Administration, 178-181, 205
Victoria, 134-144
Veiled Prophet, 82
Villa Duschene, 81, 84
Voelker, Christopher, 168, 228
Vouziers, 87-89, 227
Washington University, 94, 168, 202
Webber, Christopher, 37
Weekly, Mrs. Edward D., 83
Werner, Anne Desloge, 87-88
Werner, Mrs. Louis, II, 83, 95
Werner, Rusty, and Mark, 157, 164-165, 169, 178, 229
Westborough Country Club, 82
Westminster College, 94
Willis, Mary, 169
Woodward and Tiernan, 58
WRTH Radio, 95
Zarzuela.net, 37